Loveable

EMBRACING WHAT IS TRUEST ABOUT YOU,

SO YOU CAN TRULY EMBRACE YOUR LIFE

KELLY FLANAGAN

ZONDERVAN®

ZONDERVAN

Loveable
Copyright © 2017 by Kelly Flanagan

Requests for information should be addressed to:
Zondervan, *3900 Sparks Dr. SE, Grand Rapids, Michigan 49546*

ISBN 978-0-310-34516-9 (softcover)

ISBN 978-0-310-34517-6 (ebook)

Published in association with Creative Trust, Inc., www.creativetrust.com.

Cover design: *James W. Hall IV*
Interior design: *Kait Lamphere*

First printing January 2017 / Printed in the United States of America

For my little ones—Aidan, Quinn, and Caitlin—
who are teaching me how to be a kid again.

And for my wife,
who is my miracle.

The two most important days in your life
are the day you are born
and the day you find out why.

MARK TWAIN

Contents

A Glimpse Behind the Scenes 9

THE BACKSTORY: The Wound, the Search, and the Healing

1. The Original Wound 17
2. The Search for Healing in Our Relationships 24
3. The Search for Healing Through Significance 29
4. Healing in Three Acts 35

ACT ONE: Worthiness (You Are Enough)

Dear Little Ones, You Are Enough (No Matter What) 47
5. You Are What's Underneath Your Underneath 49
6. The First Breadcrumb on the Way to Your Worthiness . 55
7. Why the Secret to Being Worthy Is Doing Nothing . . 62
8. The Difference between Getting Rich
   and Living Richly 69
9. Why We Need to Quit Looking into Mirrors
   (and Become a Mirror) 75
10. The Good News That Sounds Too Good to Be True . . 82
11. What Grace Sees Underneath Your Mess 89
12. Worthiness Isn't Being Cocky (It's Being Honest) 95
13. You Are a Somebody (and So Is Everybody Else) 100

A Father's Letter to His Daughter (About the Worthiness of Everyone) 107

ACT TWO: Belonging (You Are Not Alone)

A Daddy's Letter to His Little Girl (About Her Future Husband) 111

14. Why Loneliness Happens, How We Make It Worse, and What We Can Do to Make It Better 113

15. A Castle, a Chrysalis, a Tomb, and a Bodyguard 121

16. How to Let Go of Your False Self 127

17. What If a Stiff Arm Is the Most Loving Thing You Can Give? 132

18. Maybe Heaven Really Is in Our Midst 137

19. The One Sentence That Can Disarm Any Bully 143

20. The Most Painful Part of Finding Belonging 149

21. When Announcing Yourself Means Announcing Your Need 155

22. Why Belonging Is Another Beginning 161

A Father's Letter to His Son (about the Only Good Reason to Get Married) 166

ACT THREE: Purpose (You Matter)

Words from a Father to His Daughter (from the Makeup Aisle) . . 171

23. The Thing You Never Knew You Always Wanted to Do 174

24. The Question That Can Silence Any Story 183

25. Why Backward Is the New Forward 189

26. Courage Isn't a Character Trait (It's a Direction) 196

27. Why There Was No Crowd at the Foot of the Cross . . 203

28. The Redemptive Relationship Between Passion, Pain, and Purpose 209

29. A Peace That Surpasses All Understanding......... 217
*A Last Letter to My Little Ones (in Case I'm Not Around
    for the Important Moments)*........................ 224
Seasons, Sequels, and Souls............................ 227

Acknowledgments................................... 233
Sources.. 237

A Glimpse Behind the Scenes

*Happy is he who still loves something that he
loved in the nursery: he has not been broken in
two by time; he is not two men, but one, and
has saved not only his soul but his life.*

G. K. CHESTERTON

In a way, I guess, the writing of this book began with a coffeepot. And a typo.

A few years ago, our old coffeemaker finally gave up the ghost, and we replaced it with a newer model featuring a bunch of buttons, a ceramic carafe, and no hot plate. According to the advertising, the carafe was so state-of-the-art it could keep the coffee hot without assistance. Like magic.

It was not magical.

The first pot of coffee was lukewarm. So was the second. By the third pot of tepid brew, my wife and I were turning to Google for answers. I intended to type "how to keep coffee hot," but accidentally typed "how to keep h," and before I could finish my question, Google autocompleted my search: "how to keep him interested." Curious, I hit enter, and was greeted by countless articles about how to be sexy and subservient, when to bring him a sandwich and when to bring him a drink And most of them were written by *women*.

Suddenly, *I* was a little hot.

My daughter, Caitlin, was three years old at the time, and I imagined her as a young woman, searching the internet for ways to keep her boyfriend or her husband interested in her, only to discover it would require her body and her obedience. I imagined how sad and lonely she would feel as she read those articles, and I wanted her to know she is worthy of interest—and of a husband who *knows* she is worthy of interest—regardless of how she looks or what she does. So I wrote Caitlin a letter and, when I read it to my wife, it brought tears to her eyes. I had intended the words for my daughter, but it turned out my wife also needed to hear them. So I thought others might need to hear them as well.

I posted the letter to my blog, and within a week it went viral.

The second time I wrote a letter to Caitlin, I was standing in a makeup aisle. Several weeks earlier, a friend had texted me from a different makeup aisle. He had a young daughter too, and he said he was disturbed by the many messages about beauty surrounding him there. He said it felt oppressive. I wanted to understand what he was feeling, so I visited a beauty aisle myself.

As I stood in the aisle, I knew *exactly* what he was feeling.

Again, I imagined Caitlin, a decade older, standing in that same aisle, absorbing all the messages suggesting her worthiness is dependent on her prettiness. I wanted to challenge the voices of the beauty industry with the voice of a father, telling her that beauty isn't something she starts putting on her face in adolescence; it's something that was put into her soul from the very *beginning.* I wanted her to know worthiness isn't something you buy in a store; it's something you discover within yourself.

So I sat down in the aisle, pulled out my laptop, and wrote Caitlin a second letter.

When I got home, I read it to my wife and, once again, she

cried. So, once again, I posted the letter to my blog. This time, it went so viral that Caitlin and I ended up on the *TODAY* show. In the wake of our television appearance, I began asking myself why the world was so eager to hear the words I was writing to her. And slowly, it began to dawn on me: it's not just little girls who need to be reminded of their inner beauty—*all* of us need to be reminded of our worthiness and the power we have to live beautiful lives.

It turns out, there is a little one in all of us.

The little one inside of you is your truest self—the you who existed before things got confusing, before guys started telling you that you had to bring them a sandwich to be interesting, before an industry started telling you that you had to buy a product to be beautiful, before you had to be tough to be enough, before you had to be cool to survive in school. The little one inside of you is the you who is most aware of your worthiness. But it is also your most wounded you, because that little boy or girl was on the front lines when the world started telling you that you weren't enough.

Recently, our oldest child, Aidan, who is in middle school, walked up to me and, out of nowhere, said, "Dad, I wish I could remember what I was like when I was a little kid." When I asked him why, he said, "Because then I'd know who I really am. Middle school takes that away from you."

There is a worthy yet wounded little one in all of us.

To be honest, the love letters I write to my kids are also love letters to the little kid inside of me. The shame and loneliness and confusion I hope to ease in them are the shame and loneliness and confusion I already carry within me. As I invite my children to awaken to their worthiness, belonging, and purpose, the little one in me slowly reawakens to his own worth, place, and passion. If you're a parent, maybe you know what I'm talking about. If you're not a parent, maybe you know what I'm talking about too.

Because we all have a little one inside of us waiting on a love letter.

This book is a love letter to my children, but it is also a love letter to myself, and to you, and to anyone who has a little one inside of them waiting to be whole again. And it's a love letter written in a very specific order, because as a therapist—and as a human being who has needed some therapy of his own—I've learned over and over again that a life well lived is like a story well told: it has a certain order and progression to it. The four parts of this book reflect that story-like progression, from the *backstory* through three acts: *worthiness, belonging*, and *purpose*.

The Backstory. Over the years, I've come to believe most of what we call life is really just backstory—people, places, and pain that set the scene for our story to really begin. Here, we'll explore the frustrating and fruitless ways we spend our days trying to find worthiness *outside* of ourselves. And we'll begin to consider a blessed possibility: the time we've spent suspecting we're no good and looking for someone or something that will finally make us feel good enough is all just staging for our first act. It's the dark moment before the dawn of our awakening.

Act One: Worthiness. The first act of life, and of this book, is an invitation to pause—to stop doing and striving and proving—and to become present to ourselves once again. It's a chance to glimpse and to greet the worthy little one who has been living within us from the beginning. It's an opportunity to rest into the soul we've forgotten—this good and beautiful thing we were before life started convincing us we were something else. It's a long and slow embrace of the worthiness we've possessed all along.

Act Two: Belonging. Having begun to embrace our true self once again, we begin to make ourselves truly known to the world. In other words, we start risking the loneliness of rejection, because the loneliness of never being authentically known is a far worse fate. Here, we will envision how, when we love and live from our true self, our relationships and communities are transformed from places of escalating conflict into places of enduring connection. Here, we will envision what it looks like to become unlonely.

Act Three: Purpose. The third act of life is made possible by the first two. Now, with clarity about who we are and support from the people around us, it's possible to spend our days awakening to the passions that have been hibernating somewhere deep inside us all along. Here, we will imagine the challenges and opportunities that present themselves when we lean into our worthiness, lean *on* our people, and choose to do the things we long to do.

As you journey through these pages, it's important to approach this book as a love letter, not an instruction manual. It's not about getting from point A to point B so you can retire from the challenges of being human. The progression from worthiness to belonging to purpose is not something that happens once—it happens over and over again. We cycle through it. We write sequel after sequel in this story we call life until, eventually, the final page is turned. This love letter is not about finding the solution to life; it's about stepping into the ongoing *rhythm* of life.

Readers of my blog know I don't write about the six simple steps to getting anywhere or overcoming anything. Shame, loneliness, and confusion aren't typically healed by new ways of thinking and doing but by new ways of *seeing.* I'm not as interested in opening your mind to a bunch of new ideas—though there are a number of those in here—as I am to opening your *eyes* to the you who has always been inside of you and the life that has always been available to you.

Because the really good news is, once you see it, you can't *un*see it.

Mark Twain said, "The two most important days in your life

are the day you are born and the day you find out why." There is
a reason for your life. Yet you cannot truly awaken to it until you
have first loved yourself well and allowed yourself to be loved well
by others. I hope this book will initiate an awakening for you, or if
your awakening is already underway, I hope it will bring clarity to
the story you are already living. Like any awakening, it will require
patience and determination and courage and risk and a little bit of
adventure. But it will be worth it. Indeed, *you* are worth it.

Because you, dear reader, are *loveable*.

The Wound, the Search, and the Healing.

All grown-ups were children first.
(But few of them remember it.)

ANTOINE DE SAINT-EXUPÉRY

CHAPTER 1

The Original Wound

Sometimes it is necessary to
reteach a thing its loveliness.

GALWAY KINNELL

*T*he whiteboard advertised our wounds.

In Illinois, licensed clinical psychologists are required to accumulate twenty-four hours of continuing education every two years. I'd signed up for a weekend seminar about Acceptance and Commitment Therapy—a cutting-edge cognitive-behavioral therapy—figuring I could complete half my hours in just two days. Continuing education classes are typically tedious and boring and not terribly educational.

The weekend of the whiteboard wasn't typical . . .

The instructors begin the seminar by telling us we will be learning the therapy by *experiencing* the therapy. So we start with breathing exercises and periods of silent, mindful reflection. During one exercise, we identify painful words and phrases that have become embedded in our core, and then one of the instructors asks us to say our words out loud as she writes them on a whiteboard. What emerges is a breathtaking array of pain encapsulated in two words: *not enough.* We are a roomful of psychologists who feel not smart enough, not attractive enough, not tall enough, not successful enough, not popular enough, not influential enough, not powerful enough, not strong enough, not *anything* enough. What words are embedded like shrapnel in my soul?

Not interesting enough. Boring, forgettable, expendable.

Gazing at the words on the whiteboard, I'm beginning to wonder if there is something emotionally toxic in the Chicago drinking water when the instructor reaches up and pulls down a movie screen. After tapping a few keys on her laptop, she projects a photo of another whiteboard onto the screen. The words are arranged differently and written in different colors, but they are all there—the same not-enough words—on a different whiteboard in a different state.

When she taps the keys again, the image of still *another* whiteboard appears. This one had been captured in a different country. Another tap. Another whiteboard. A different *continent*. She and her colleague had conducted the same seminar in widely diverse settings around the world, and yet they still mined the same not-enough words from the hearts of human beings everywhere. Apparently, at least one thing is universal: we all share an experience so powerful and ubiquitous it has wrapped its invasive tendrils all the way around our bruised and broken planet.

It's called shame.

For millennia, the word *shame* has connoted dishonor and disrepute. Still today, we tend to think of shame as a rare, complicated, and disgraceful emotion. But shame is not rare; it is actually quite common, even universal. And shame is not terribly complicated either. Shame is simply the belief we are not enough. It is the core conviction that we are without sufficient value—that we have somehow fallen short of this thing called worthiness. This belief then takes many forms, including thoughts and feelings, and it is most palpable as a haunting whisper issuing from the shadowy corners of our mind, telling us life is a test that we're failing and a competition that we're losing. Usually, the whisper has been there so long, we don't experience it as a deceptive intruder distorting our reality. Instead, we experience it as our trusted *narrator*—the familiar voice in our head, telling us the truth about who we are. So, when it tells us we are less than enough, we believe it.

However, at the center of every human being is a spark of God—a smoldering ember of the divine—and regardless of the mess we make of things, the wreck we make of our lives, our insecurities and doubts and fears and mistakes and transgressions, nothing can extinguish it. We are, each of us, a uniquely embodied soul made in the image of God, and that part of us cannot be unmade. The dictionary defines *worthy* as "having adequate value." As the living, breathing bearers of the eternal, transcendent, and limitless Love that spun the planets and hung the stars, we qualify. And then some. The foundational truth of our humanity is that we are worthy enough to participate in this "cosmic dance," as author and Trappist monk Thomas Merton calls it. It is this truth that our shame relentlessly calls into question.

Shame whispers in all of us, and it usually begins whispering *early*, which is why I call it our "original wound." Most of us first experience it sometime in toddlerhood, before we're old enough to decide what we let into our tender hearts and what we keep out. If we were mistreated or abused in our early years, the doubts about our worthiness are likely to become central to our identity—we don't know who we are without them. But even if we lived a fairy-tale life—and some of us do—we are never completely spared from the effects of shame because, somewhere along the way, someone whose opinion mattered to us failed to reflect the worthiness within us.

For instance, I'd like to believe middle school is entirely responsible for Aidan beginning to forget who he is, but I know, despite my best efforts, I've played a part in wounding him too. He is a free spirit, much more like his mother than like me. He is always forgetting something or misplacing something or leaving something unfinished. And I regularly express—in both subtle and not so subtle ways—my disappointment that he is not as meticulous as me. Disappointment is the most common delivery system for shame, like a Trojan horse you roll into a kid's heart. When night falls, shame climbs out. I love my son, but I've unintentionally rolled Trojan horses into his heart. When a parent or a friend—or anyone we look to for our sense of identity—expresses disappointment with who we are, the Trojan horse rolls in.

None of us emerge from childhood unscathed.

Is it any wonder, then, that the symptoms of shame are everywhere? Is it any wonder we compete for worthiness in virtually everything we do? When kids form cliques. When bullies bully. When teenagers compete on athletic fields as if they're battlefields. When young girls dress seductively. When young boys flex their muscles and their machismo. When we chase careers like our salvation depends on the next promotion. When we covet a certain house in a certain neighborhood as proof we've "arrived." When we dread being known, yet fear being forgotten. When we bury our mistakes, and our feelings. When we look out at the world from behind the masks we wear and wonder if we measure up.

Almost daily, my three kids come to me competing for my approval, angling for the experience of worthiness they think I can bestow. They act as if worthiness is a scarce resource for which they must search—like hidden, colored eggs on Easter morning. They think they must find it somewhere outside of themselves and fill their baskets with it, and they fear someone else will get to it first.

Their shame is already obscuring the truth: worthiness is the *least* scarce resource in the universe. It has been lavished abundantly upon all of us. It can't be given *to* us; it can only be glimpsed *within* us. But my kids are human, so I expect they'll do what the rest of us are doing: they'll live their own backstories, exhibiting all the usual symptoms of shame, trying to overcome it in so many frustratingly futile ways.

The weekend of the whiteboard is nearing its conclusion as one of the instructors guides us through a final exercise. We sit in silence, close our eyes, and breathe slowly. I hear a few muffled sobs and sniffles from around the room. We've learned a lot about the therapy and our shame, and almost everyone is feeling a little fragile. I haven't shed a tear though.

I'm pretty proud of myself.

The instructor asks us to envision standing outside our childhood home. "Imagine you are once again the age you were when you lived in that place," he says. I imagine the house we lived in when I was eleven.

"Look down at yourself," the instructor continues. "Notice your knobby knees. Open the door to the house. Notice your small hand on the door handle. Once inside, take in the sights and sounds and smells of your history. Then go to the room where you're most likely to find your mother. Ask her for what you need from her." I go to the kitchen. I want to ask her for a hug.

I ask her for an orange instead.

Because when you fear you're not interesting enough and believe you're a burden, you find ways to compensate. I compensate by making as little trouble as possible. By being a good boy. By being convenient. By asking people only for things I know they can easily give. Even in my own imagination.

I'm still not crying, and I'm still proud of myself.

"Now go to the room where you're most likely to find your father," the instructor says. "Ask him for what you need from him." I imagine my dad is in the living room watching television. I want him to reassure me I'm becoming a man, and a *good* man at that. I consider standing in front of the television to get his attention, but I've been told I make a better door than a window, and I don't want to block his view. Again, I refrain from asking for what I need, and when the instructor tells us to leave the house and walk back outside, I do so happily. No tears. Still proud.

Except the exercise isn't over.

"Walk out onto the road in front of your house," he says, "and you'll see someone off in the distance walking toward you. This is your adult self." I watch the distant figure as he gets closer and finally stands in front of me. It's the me I am now, looking at fifth-grade me, and he sees right past all my accommodating behavior. He *knows*. He sees the fear that I'm not interesting enough, that I'll be abandoned, that I won't make it on my own in this scary and uncertain world. And as the instructor begins to speak again, I know it's coming—the same instruction as before: "Now ask your adult self for what you need from him or her." Suddenly, I can't hold back the tears. "Please," I say to adult me, "just tell me I'm okay and I'm going to be okay." And adult me squats down. He takes fifth-grade me gently by the shoulders, looks me directly in the eyes, and says, "Kelly, you *are* okay, and you are going to *be* okay."

Sometimes it is necessary to reteach a thing its loveliness, indeed.

Maybe you're like me and that room full of psychologists and the world full of people represented by the not-enough words on the whiteboards. Maybe, over the years, you've come to believe your mistakes and failures and disappointments and loneliness are the only true things about you. Maybe, like me, you are needing to relearn what is *truest* about you. Maybe you, too, need to rediscover what you are made of despite the messes you've made. Maybe your whole life is an invitation to get reacquainted with that divine spark at the center of you, to blow on the embers, to fan the flames. Until one day you begin to hear within you echoes of your worthiness, echoes resounding with the truth:

You *are* okay, and you are going to *be* okay.

CHAPTER 2

The Search for Healing in Our Relationships

We must be our own before we can be another's.

RALPH WALDO EMERSON

When shame tells us we're not good enough, we do the natural thing—we start searching for worthiness elsewhere. And there are two places we search for it most: the people in our lives and the purpose of our lives. Let's talk about people first, because that's usually where we search first. Having been wounded by people, we seek to be healed by them as well. But it rarely works. Because the search for worthiness is not a group project.

I'm making the bed and grumbling because, once again, the sheets and blankets have all been pulled to my wife's side of the bed. I've spent another cold, winter night clinging to the edge of the bedding, fighting for scraps. As I pull up the sheets, nursing my habitual resentment, suddenly it hits me: last night my wife slept in a bed almost a thousand miles away. The day before, she and the kids had left town for a vacation. They're gone and I'm home alone.

I've been married for almost fourteen years and, for all of those fourteen years, I've blamed my wife for stealing the covers. Fourteen years can't be wrong, can they?

I decide this one night was a fluke. I finish making the bed and assume it's still true—my wife is a hoarder of warmth and I've been the sleeping, shivering collateral damage. Until the next morning, when I awake to discover the same thing. And the morning after that. And the next. Apparently, my wife doesn't pull the covers to her side. Apparently, I *push* them.

It makes me wonder how much of what I blame on my wife is not really her fault at all. How many times, for instance, have I accused her of stealing my worthiness away from me, and how many times was I actually *giving* it away, like bedcovers on a cold night? How many times have I acted like it's her job to make me feel good enough? How many times have I searched for my worthiness in the way she looks at me or responds to me or thinks about me, instead of searching for it in the only place it can be found—*inside* of me?

As a therapist, I've watched it happen over and over again, as well-intentioned people unwittingly push the responsibility for healing the wounds of their hearts onto the people they love. We expect others to rescue us from our shame. We demand others fix our feelings of unworthiness. After all, we experience our original wound in our earliest, most vulnerable relationships, so why wouldn't we expect our subsequent relationships to heal it?

So, having our enough-ness thrown into question by the people we love most, we venture out into the world and embark on a search for love and acceptance, hoping someone out there will restore our sense of worthiness. We seek it from our friends and teachers and peers and coaches and boyfriends and girlfriends and lovers and coworkers and bosses and even strangers on the street. We look for it in everyone.

In fact, it's the most common reason for getting married.

Most of us believe our search for worthiness ends on our wedding day. Ultimately, we don't make a lifelong commitment to someone because they make us feel loved; we commit to them because, for a time, they have made us feel *loveable*. We think we have found the person who will, at last, make us feel forever worthy. But a marriage can't bear the burden of our search for worthiness. No relationship can.

The Greatest Commandment declares, "Love your neighbor as yourself." Why does self-love come first? Because when we try to love someone else before we have first embraced what is loveable in ourselves, our love *for* them inevitably devolves into an ongoing effort to get *from* them the kind of love we imagine will make us feel worthy. Then even our most sincere attempts at love turn into manipulation. At best, we give love in order to get love, which turns love into a commodity, and a cheapened one at that. At worst, we try to coerce love from one another in a million little ways. Personally, I prefer listing the ways my wife has disappointed me, screwed up her priorities, or treated someone else better than she has treated me. Of course, I do so passive-aggressively, so I can deny it if she calls me out.

When we're searching for our worthiness in the person to whom we've committed, it can quickly become the central struggle of the relationship. Some of us resign ourselves to this lifelong drama. Others tire of it and go searching for worthiness in other people. Sometimes we look for it in our children: we might bend over backward to earn their approval or we might use the worthwhile things they do—trophies, honor rolls, Ivy League degrees, and impressive careers—as proof of our own worthiness. Sometimes we look for our worthiness in affairs. Sometimes we just get divorced and begin the search again in a second marriage. There's a reason second marriages have an even higher rate of divorce: the search never ends well.

Like I said, the quest for worthiness is not a group project.

Several days into my family's vacation, I'm in my home office writing, the bedcovers forgotten, when I hear a strange crackling noise coming from the bedroom. I follow the sound and find our dog on the bed, gnawing on a Cadbury egg. My wife had left my favorite Easter candy underneath my pillow as a surprise—a gift to remind me I'm loved and *loveable*. What I'd failed to discover, even after sleeping on it, the dog had sniffed out.

As he looks up at me with puppy-guilt in his shiny eyes, I feel tears well up in my own, and fourteen years of mornings flash before them. My wife is not responsible for hoarding the covers, and she is not responsible for the doubts I have about my worthiness. They existed long before I even knew *she* existed. And in fact, she's been trying to reteach me my loveliness for fourteen years. But even after fourteen years, I don't see it. I'm still much more likely to grumble about the covers than I am to search beneath them for a gift.

Shame is a wound that pours salt on itself.

When I believe I'm unworthy, I expect the covers of life to be pulled away from me. I expect to be left cold and alone, and my expectations become a self-fullfilling prophecy, because I fail to recognize the reminders of my worthiness being offered by the ones who love me. Then I blame them for not loving me well. But the truth is, it's up to me to recognize such gifts when they've been offered. It's up to me to open them and to savor them.

It's up to each of us.

In most relationships, we show up on the other's doorstep with an open wound of shame, and some people will add salt to the wound, while other people apply salve and a bandage. In other words, some people continue to shame us, while others see our worthiness and give us grace—the kind of grace that sees the good in us even when we can't see it in ourselves. Without a doubt, my wife is a salve-and-bandage kind of person. The question is, will I allow her to apply her balm? Will I allow the grace with which she sees me to change the way *I* see me?

Or will I complain she's not doing it well enough?

Loving yourself well—embracing your foundational worthiness—is a prerequisite for allowing yourself to *be loved* well by someone else. Until you can see your worthiness for yourself, you won't be able to see it through the eyes of anyone else, either. No matter how long you search for the right pair of eyes. Reclaiming your worthiness—and living from it—is your responsibility. You can take it back.

Like missing bedcovers after a long, cold night.

— CHAPTER 3 —

The Search for Healing through Significance

In the middle of the journey of our life
I came to myself in a dark wood
where the straight way was lost.

DANTE ALIGHIERI

On March 8, 2014, Malaysian Airlines Flight 370 disappeared less than an hour after takeoff. Based on its final satellite communications and some complicated math, officials determined the airplane went down somewhere over the southern Indian Ocean. This focused the search within a relatively small area. After scouring the ocean floor and finding nothing, the search began expanding in ever-widening circles. Years later, the plane is, tragically, still missing.

This is how our search for worthiness works, too, when we continue to search outside of ourselves.

Initially, we believe we will find our worthiness within the relatively confined territory of our relationships. But when the search comes up empty, we start expanding it into the rest of life. Our search for worthiness ripples outward in concentric circles as we try to prove our worth through influence, impact, and significance—by making a name for ourselves, we hope to make ourselves worthy. Our shame tells us that by doing something that matters, *we* will finally matter.

However, when you are walking around with a spark of God within you—when you have been created and deemed very good, when you have been intentionally knit together in your mother's womb, when you are called the light of the world and the salt of the earth—you already count, simply because you're living, breathing, and awake. In fact, that ultimately *is* our purpose: to stop sleepwalking and to start doing what makes us fully alive, fully *alight*. Of course, in the midst of our shame, that sounds too good to be true. So, instead, we keep widening the scope of our search for worthiness, with nothing to show for it.

He leans forward in his chair, one foot tapping the floor rapidly.

Jaw clenched.

Head bowed.

He's in his early twenties, born and raised in a well-to-do household in an affluent Chicago suburb. He attended an elite high school and then, following in his father's footsteps, completed a business degree at an excellent college and is poised to find a prestigious sales job. His path seems clear, and extraordinary. However, he has no interest in sales.

So, on this afternoon, he's in my office, plagued by insecurity, weighed down by loneliness, and utterly confused about the trajectory of his life. In a moment of exasperated honesty, his agitation boils over into a question: "Have you ever felt like we're all on this big rock hurtling through space and no one has any idea what the *heck* is going on?" He looks up at me and, despite his best efforts to keep his emotions in check, his eyes are brimming with tears. In the midst of his life's journey, he finds himself waking in a dark wood. He is Dante in tennis shoes.

When we turn our purpose into another search for worthiness, the straight way is easily lost.

While shopping recently, I came across a T-shirt emblazoned with the phrase "Be More." In the store, it struck me as inspirational, so I bought it. But when I wore it to a friend's holiday party two days later, I had second thoughts. As I greeted people, I put myself in their shoes. Be *more*. In other words, "Who you are is not enough; we need more from you." Sometimes when we aim for inspiration, we deliver humiliation instead.

Life is often painful and messy. It's blood-sweat-and-tears messy. It's frustration and anxiety and sadness and embarrassment messy. It can be tragic and unpredictable. It spins us around, flips us upside down, and disorients us. Sometimes daily. In the midst of this wild and messy life, it's no wonder we feel like our lives depend on making some sense of the chaos. In a way, they *do* depend on us making meaning from it all. To live fully and to love fiercely—and those just might be the same thing—we have to ask, "Why am I here? What am I here to do? What is my purpose?"

Yet in the dark wood of our shame, where the straight way has been lost, we tend to answer those questions with T-shirt slogans—Be More—and motivational clichés: leave a legacy, be a difference maker, make an impact. Our shame tells us that to be enough, we must be *more* than enough; to live an acceptable life, we must live an *extraordinary* life. So, it shuts us down. Daunted by our own lofty expectations, many of us give up before we even begin. Others of us do begin, but our sense of worthiness becomes fused with the outcome of our endeavors—our successes become a compulsive and exhausting exercise in proving ourselves, and our failures turn into self-loathing and disillusionment.

In our efforts to make a big splash, we eventually drown.

Recently, Caitlin started taking the piano lessons she's been begging to begin for more than a year. After one of her first practice sessions, she came to me and observed, with the innocence of a little one, "Daddy, it's really hard to play the piano when you're thinking about how happy your momma and daddy are that you're playing the piano." I wish I'd had that kind of insight when I was six. Perhaps I did. Perhaps we all did, and we forgot. Remembering it would have saved me a lot of searching because, like playing the piano, it's awfully hard to live a life of purpose when you're thinking about how significant your purpose must be. In the end, ironically, our quest to matter gets in the way of doing the things that matter to us most.

I look into the eyes of Dante in Tennis Shoes and tell him the truth—I know exactly how he feels. I tried to "be more" by earning academic degrees. I thought when I transitioned from a small town high school to a Big Ten university I would find my purpose in the world. I didn't. So I tried again. I entered a graduate program at another Big Ten university. I didn't find the answers there either. So I assumed when I achieved the summit of academic degrees—a doctorate in philosophy—all the confusing things within me would fall into place. They didn't. I fell into a depression the year after I earned my doctorate because nothing in me had changed and there were no more degrees to pursue. I awoke in a dark wood where the straight way of academic achievement had been lost.

I was Dante in Khakis.

So I look at him and tell him I know what it's like to carry the burden of extraordinariness, which shame places on our shoulders. I know what it's like to believe you must meet and exceed your parents' expectations, or at least their example. I know what it's like to think you're supposed to be a superhero in your own story, mastering life's challenges in a series of effortless leaps and bounds, and making a name for yourself in the process. I tell him none of us can bear this burden of the extraordinary.

Yet before we embrace our worthiness, we mistakenly believe we must.

I look at Dante in Tennis Shoes and simplify things with a question: "Do you love yourself? Now. Exactly the way you are. Ordinary you. Do you love yourself?" His puddled eyes overflow as he slowly, almost imperceptibly, shakes his head from side to side. So I say as gently as I can, "You have to let something sink deeply into your soul and, until you do, we're not going to talk about your purpose or even your job. Those things can't bear the weight of your search to find worthiness in extraordinariness." And then I tell him the most important thing I've learned about purpose:

There is loveliness in *ordinariness.*

What is your purpose?

The question reflects a holy impulse written into your very DNA. Human beings are meaning-making creatures. When you yearn to know why you're here, you are honoring the very essence of your humanity. We are here to live with intention and purpose. But your shame will always answer questions about purpose with a dangling carrot. Shame will tell you what you must do in order to matter, and then, once you do it, it will tell you what *else* you must do.

The carrot will always remain just out of reach.

Therefore, it's important to pause the purpose question until you can trust this to be true: you don't need to be *more*; you just need to be more *you*. You're here to play the piano you've been dying to play, and you are free to stop thinking about how much it matters and to whom. You're here, simply, to play the music you hear inside of you until you are wide awake and fully alive—until being human finally feels like the gift it is.

Yes, your searching has led you astray at times. Your path has not been straight. You've meandered. There have been sinkholes and quicksand and booby traps along the way. You've taken detours and you've gotten turned around from time to time.

That's okay; your wandering isn't you.

Instead, every time you get a little lost, it's a chance to find your way back to the you that you've always been, though sometimes forgotten. In the returning, you will get to know yourself a little better, and you will see your purpose a little more clearly. That's how it works—that's how you find the path out of your dark wood.

These days, I don't feel so much like Dante in Khakis, and I don't feel like Superman in Khakis either. These days, I feel like Kelly in Khakis. And that is enough. Because you don't need to be extraordinary to be somebody.

It's okay to be ordinary you.

— CHAPTER 4 —

Healing in Three Acts

It takes courage to grow up and
become who you really are.

E. E. CUMMINGS

I intentionally waited to read the Harry Potter books until the last one was published. For months, I avoided all press around the launching of the seventh book. I shunned social media, left the room when friends discussed the book, and told my wife I'd divorce her if she so much as mentioned Professor Snape. I didn't want to experience the final scenes of that epic tale before I had experienced the rest of the story. I knew I'd lose something important if that happened—something I'd never be able to get back. Because a story needs to unfold in its intended order.

That's why, when you're flipping through television channels and stumble across the last scene of a movie you've always wanted to see, you quickly change the channel, preserving the entire story for another time. That's why you plug your ears when a friend starts talking about the new season of a television show when you're still in the middle of the previous season on Netflix. That's why, when the cashier casually mentions who won the big game you were about to go home and watch on DVR, you go home and delete it instead. Movies and television shows and big games are stories, and knowing the conclusion before we've experienced the beginning and the middle of the tale spoils the whole journey. It's the reason we demand spoiler alerts.

Now, perhaps you are one of those people who flips to the end of a book to find out the ending before you even begin. If so, I understand. I really do. Waiting to find out how the whole mess turns out can be an excruciating, tension-riddled journey. Much like life, in fact. But next time, I encourage you to wait. Because the beauty of a good ending can only be truly appreciated if you've first fallen in love with the characters and then joined them in their peril. We've been given stories so our souls might have endless opportunities for delight, and our souls are most delighted when the story progresses in a particular order—the setup, the confrontation, and the resolution.

The Setup. In this first act, we get to know the characters. We come alongside them in the story they are telling with their lives, and we begin to care about them, pull for them, even love them. The setup usually ends in a dramatic moment called an "inciting incident." It is the point of no return in a story. The inciting incident fundamentally alters the way the key characters experience themselves and their lives. Suddenly, they see what they couldn't see before. A veil has been lifted, and they've gotten a glimpse of their story from an entirely new angle. For the first time, they begin to have clarity about what they want—or don't want—and it is this vision that propels them into the second act.

The Confrontation. In the second act, the protagonist encounters tension and conflict. Hopes and dreams are in doubt. Peril and pain are a fire that refines the character's integrity, while threatening to melt it. In the midst of these trials, we begin to see the demons the protagonist must face in order to survive and to thrive in the third and final act.

The Resolution. In the resolution, the dramatic tension of the character's story is resolved in a climactic moment—Rocky Balboa stays on his feet, Luke Skywalker blows up the Death Star, and Dorothy douses the Wicked Witch. (I know I've just become the cashier at the supermarket, spoiling the end of several good stories for you, but those stories are all more than thirty years old, and I'm pretty sure the statute of limitations on spoiler alerts is a quarter of a century.)

It is essential for us to understand the sequential progression of a good story, not only so we can enjoy our books and movies and games to the fullest, but so we can live our *lives* to the fullest as well. You see, life—your life—is meant to be a good story too, and in order for it to have the meaning and beauty and joy you want it to have, it needs to progress sequentially through three acts of its own: worthiness, belonging, and purpose.

But shame interferes with the natural unfolding of our lives.

It tricks us into telling our stories out of order. Our lives are meant to flow from the worthiness we discover in our first act. But when shame tells us there is no worthiness in us, we move on to the second act and search for worthiness in belonging, or skip right to the third act to find worthiness in our life's purpose. Disrupting the proper order has consequences—confusion, apathy, loneliness, codependency, violence, jealousy, cynicism, burnout, hopelessness, and despair, to name a few.

And yet.

Every moment is an opportunity to turn all of that disorder into backstory, by stepping with fear and trembling and courage and intentionality into your first act. In other words, every moment is an opportunity to tell a story—to live a life—that begins with worthiness.

ACT ONE: Worthiness (You Are Enough)

A few years ago, an Icelandic tour bus driver contacted police to report that a foreign tourist had gone missing. The driver described the woman as "Asian, about 160 cm [five foot three], in dark clothing, and speaks English well." Fifty members of the tour group set out on foot to look for the woman. In all the confusion, it turned out the reportedly missing woman was actually a member of the search party! She had changed her clothing at a rest stop, and the bus driver no longer recognized her. Unbeknownst to her, she was searching for herself. Later, the woman would say she didn't recognize the description of herself.

Few of us do.

If I told you about someone who is gloriously messy, beautifully weak, breathtakingly strong, lovely and good and whole and holy, would you recognize this description of who you already are? Most of us don't, so we abandon our first act and go searching for ourselves in second-act relationships and third-act purpose. But we won't find ourselves there either, because, like the woman on the Icelandic tour bus, we're searching for a self that was never really lost to begin with.

I have a friend who spent years searching for her worthiness in all sorts of painful and self-destructive ways. Her backstory was filled with shame and confusion, until an inciting incident plunged her into a deep and total experience of her own worthiness. Inciting incidents can come in many guises. Her inciting incident was a dream.

In the dream, the scenes of her story rolled by—all of her regrettable decisions and mistakes. As she watched her life flash before her slumbering eyes, her shame began to crescendo. Until, suddenly, she noticed she wasn't alone in the dream. Offstage, God was watching, smiling softly, and repeatedly whispering, "One less day. One less day. One less day. One less day." One less day until she remembers who she is. One less day until she remembers she is *enough*. One less day until she realizes there is nothing to search for. One less day until she awakens to her worthiness.

Ironically, our awakening can happen even while we're asleep.

It can happen at *any* moment if, in that moment, you realize your searching will always be in vain because you have been searching for a you that was never really missing. This is the moment in which you embrace what is truest about you: you've been loveable all along. This moment—this experience—becomes your True North; though you can and *will* get distracted again, you will never again be without a way to reorient yourself. After your inciting incident, you will, finally, recognize the description of yourself.

ACT TWO: Belonging (You Are Not Alone)

I wish every life story could be a one-act story. I wish we could experience our enough-ness and rest there peacefully for the remainder of our lives. But there is no such thing as a one-act story, and meaningful and satisfying one-act *lives* don't exist either. While worthiness is the foundation of our story, life is about more than just embracing ourselves; it's also about being embraced *by* others and becoming an embracer *of* others. In other words, life isn't just about worthiness. Life is also about finding a place of belonging in the world.

We need to find our chosen family—the people who will have our back when the rest of the world doesn't. We need people who can be mirrors, reflecting back to us the truth about who we really are, even when we're having trouble seeing it ourselves. We need pockets of community, safe harbors where we can find shelter from the tumultuous storms of life. And those people—*your* people—*are* out there. They're just waiting for you to announce yourself.

In your first act, you recognize your true self; in your second act, you *reveal* it.

The problem is, revealing your true self feels dangerous. Philosopher-theologian Peter Rollins tells a parable that illustrates the peril we face as we enter the second act of life. A panic-stricken man contacted a psychoanalyst because he was tormented by a peculiar malady: he thought he was seed on the ground. The psychoanalyst treated him five times a week for several years, until both agreed he was cured—he finally knew who he really was. Several weeks later, though, the psychoanalyst got a frantic call from the man, who cried, "Doctor, new neighbors have moved in next door! And they have chickens!" Confused, the psychoanalyst asked, "But you know you're not seed, right?" To which the man responded, "Of course *I* know I'm not seed. But do the *chickens* know?"

It's dangerous to announce ourselves, because there are chickens out there who won't treat us like we're worthy. We run the risk of getting pecked to pieces. Being openly ourselves is a gamble, so most of us hedge our bets by announcing another self—a false self. It's like a layer of armor, protecting us against a world that might try to eat us alive. And a little armor can't hurt, can it?

Except it can, and it does.

We can't find authentic belonging by pretending and protecting and perfecting. When our true self remains hidden and unknown, we become lonelier than ever, even, for instance, in the longest of friendships and the most committed of marriages. In the second act of life, we decide whether or not to step out from behind our facade into the open space of vulnerability, in order to find authentic belonging. In other words, the "confrontation" in our second act is not just a confrontation with a dangerous world, but also with our own false self.

The ultimate confrontation occurs *within* us, over and over again.

It happens the moment you realize you've always done what people have wanted you to do and you've always said what people have wanted to hear, but now you don't want to do and say those things anymore. Do you keep protecting your heart or start revealing it?

It happens the moment you want to tell those you love about the depth of your love for them, but you hesitate because you can't know for sure if it will be reciprocated. So what do you do? Do you protect your heart or reveal it?

It happens the moment you realize some of your anger has been justified, but mostly it has been a way of keeping people at arm's length. Do you keep protecting your heart with it, or start revealing your heart *without* it?

It happens the moment you realize you've treated your whole life like one long first date, telling yourself you've been putting your best foot forward when really you've been putting your *false* foot forward—and now you are surrounded by people who like the *advertisement* of you rather than the *actual* you. Do you keep protecting your heart, or start revealing it?

Protection versus revelation. This is the dramatic tension in the second act of life. Will we settle for the faux belonging of the false self, or will we find the people to whom we truly belong by courageously announcing the loveable person we've discovered ourselves to be? If we choose not to shy away from this internal confrontation, the refining fire of vulnerability will further clarify our sense of who we are and what we are passionate about doing in the world, and we will draw nearer to the people who will stand beside us as we practice our passions.

ACT THREE: Purpose (You Matter)

Last Christmas, I attended a concert at my son's school of music. Early in the show, a group of boys and girls got up from the front row and gathered around a table full of handbells. One child was in a wheelchair. Several hobbled. One set of hands was twisted and gnarled. I checked the program—they were students from a music school for children with severe physical and mental disabilities. They were there to play "Silent Night."

Slowly, each child picked up one handbell. Then their instructor faced them and pointed at the children in turn, signaling each one to play his or her note at the appointed time. If a child failed to do so, she waited patiently, pointing and smiling gently until his or her note was played, and then she went on to the next child. By the time they finished, there wasn't a dry eye in the house. It was a holy moment. And it is the answer to the big *why* question we face in the third act of our lives: Why are we here?

We are here to play our one note.

Sometimes, we sense this big God-finger pointing at us, and we tend to assume it's accusing us of something, or disappointed in us, or telling us we have to do something bigger and better. But that perception is a projection of our shame and insecurity and confusion. The finger of God is more like that of the gentle music instructor. God is simply smiling, telling us it's our turn, and waiting patiently for us to play the one note that only we can play.

"At the heart of the universe is a smile," writes author Philip Yancey, "a pulse of joy passed down from the moment of creation."

God is not demanding something *from* us and is not disappointed *in* us. Rather, God is smiling upon us and *waiting* on us, not merely to do the right thing or to be more obedient, but to play our one note. You are part of a big, beautiful work of music called humanity. When God gestures in your direction, it's your cue, and all you have to do is play your note. Inadequacy is impossible.

But what is your note?

If you're like most of us, you probably feel like you don't have a clue how to answer that question. But the truth is, you have much more than a clue—in fact, you likely already know the answer. We ultimately know the note we want to play, but shame makes us doubt it for a while—it tells us our one note is not enough. Which is why it is essential to live the first two acts of our story before we ask why we are here—once we trust we're enough no matter what we do, and once we trust the embrace of our people more than the rejection of the masses, we can trust that what we're here to do *matters*, no matter how ordinary it might seem. In the climactic moment of act three, we embrace our purpose, and begin playing our note in the great symphony of humanity that is just beginning to tune up.

A psychiatrist friend of mine recently told me growing up is like walking up a steep mountain. You can't hike straight up. It's too treacherous. You'd die of ambition. Though it takes longer, the best way to walk up a steep mountain is to circle it slowly, on a gradually ascending path. So when we circle around it, we encounter the same view as before, but it's not *quite* the same. We're viewing it from a slightly higher elevation. He said this is how life and growth and healing work.

It's how good stories work as well.

Some of our most beloved tales could not be told in a single volume. Tolkien needed three books to tell the story of Frodo and Bilbo and the ring. Lewis needed seven to tell the story of Aslan and Narnia. Rowling needed seven to tell us the tale of the Boy Who Lived. Stephen King needed seven to tell us about Roland the Gunslinger and his ka-tet. The Torah contains five books and the Bible requires sixty-six to tell God's story. In these collections, the structure of the story plays out in its totality within each individual volume. But the multiple volumes are necessary, because stories build on themselves.

Our lives, like stories, build on themselves too.

The story of your life cannot be told in a single volume. Which is to say, the first time you walk through your three acts, it will be a beautiful story unto itself, but it won't be your *whole* story. There will be more to tell. And the second time you circle the mountain, living your three acts once again, you'll be a little higher up—your sense of worthiness will deepen, your trust in your belonging will strengthen, and your clarity about your purpose will sharpen. I'm not sure how many circuits of the mountain it will require any one of us to reach the top. In fact, I'm not sure if our story is ever really completed in this lifetime. The one thing I'm sure of is this: with each circuit, we're moving *upward*.

Wherever you find yourself in your story—wherever you find yourself as you climb the mountainside of your life—this book is an invitation to walk the path with me for a while. And by the time we're done, I pray your life will feel a little less like climbing.

And a little more like *rising*.

—— *Act One:* *Worthiness* ——

You Are Enough

*Remember that you already are
what you are seeking.*

RICHARD ROHR

Dear Little Ones, You Are Enough
(No Matter What)

Dear Little Ones,

I'm sitting in a parking lot as I write this. On one side of the parking lot is a playground where kids are laughing and playing. On the other side of the parking lot is a transitional living unit for troubled youth, where kids are hurting and struggling.

On one side, the dream of every parent.

On the other side, the fear of every parent.

I've often wondered why the county would put this facility next to a park. But as I sit here today, the message seems clear: the line between our brightest dreams and our darkest fears is a fine one, isn't it? Finer than the width of this parking lot.

Little Ones, what you do *matters*. Each and every choice has a creative potential as powerful as the Force that hung the stars and spun the planets. So the fearful part of me wants to give you one more lecture about the importance of your choices. But I'm not going to do that. Instead, I want to tell you about who you are, *regardless* of the choices you make.

Regardless of which side of the street you end up on, I want you to know: your core is untarnished, your center is unaltered, your heart is unblemished, your spark is still burning, and your original identity is uncorrupted. Little Ones, regardless of your choices, I want you to know you are worthy.

You are enough.

On the day you bring home your first A and on the day you bring home your first

F. On the day you make the game-winning shot and on the day you get cut from the team. On the day you sit at the cool-kids table and on the day you eat lunch with your loneliness. On the day you get a standing ovation and on the day you freeze up and forget your lines . . .

You are enough.

On the day you resist peer pressure and on the day you give in. On the day you enter college and on the day you enter rehab. On the day you get your first promotion and on the day you get your first pink slip. On the day you run a triathlon and on the day of your diagnosis . . .

You are enough.

On the day you were born you were enough, and on the day you die you will be enough, regardless of what comes in between.

Little Ones, I'm not saying you're free from consequences. But I am telling you this: while many poor choices do have a consequence, most poor choices are already a consequence—the consequence of doubting our worthiness. The task of our lives is simply to rest into the truth of our worthiness and to walk the path of who we already are.

So, Little Ones, when you've lost your way and you wish you could do something impossible like rewind time, remember this: there is one thing that is always possible—it is always possible to return to the center of who you are. You will find there the truth of your worthiness whispered upon the tongue of grace and it will, quite simply, never steer you wrong.

To my Beloved,

Daddy

CHAPTER 5

You Are What's Underneath Your Underneath

Light will eventually split you open.

HAFIZ

W e're all pretty familiar with the first two layers of our humanity—the surface layer we present to the world and the just-below-the-surface layer we hide from the world. The surface layer is the image we seek to project, and it's usually as flawless as we can possibly make it. The other layer—the underneath—is where we keep our not-so-pristine stuff like fear, uncertainty, sadness, jealousy, confusion, anger, arrogance, and hopelessness. Usually, the underneath is uncomfortable or disturbing, so we do our best to avoid it—we stay on the surface of ourselves because we don't want to know what other troubling realities may lurk within our depths. Consequently, we never get around to digging into our underneath, and we conclude there is darkness at the bottom of our humanity. Every once in a while, though, someone keeps digging, *into* the dark underneath and *through* the dark underneath, all the way to the center of themselves.

And into the light.

Kids often start getting bullied around third or fourth grade. For Aidan, it was fourth grade. Two of the more athletic kids in the school decided to target him. Who knows how that decision gets made within a clique, but once made, it is almost impossible to undo. The targeted kid becomes the focus of the group's cruelty. It was painful to watch him suffer through it and, to be honest, I had little compassion for the chief bully. Though I knew he, too, had likely experienced bullying and was simply doing what had been done to him, I didn't much care. My protective instinct was too strong. I had crazy fantasies of confronting him and terrifying him. I'm a realist, though, and the fantasies always ended with the police at my door or his dad knocking my teeth out. So, instead, my wife and I did the grown-up thing and worked with the school to put an end to the bullying. By the end of the school year, it had mostly stopped.

A year later, Aidan was scheduled to sing a solo in the school talent show. I nervously wondered if the head bully would be in the audience and what he might do to renew the abuse. As Aidan took the stage, I scanned the audience for the kid. He was nowhere to be seen. I figured he must be home sick. Despite my best effort to be mature, I have to admit, the thought was a little satisfying.

Aidan performed beautifully and received a standing ovation, and fifteen minutes later I was glowing with pride as I walked toward the exit. But then I stopped short. Directly ahead, coming through the front door of the school was the bully, his sister, and their mother. The two children walked past me, but their mother stopped and asked how Aidan had done in the talent show. I told her he'd done great, and then, curious, I asked how she knew he'd been performing. She said her kids had to miss the show for an appointment, but Aidan was the one act they wanted to see because, they'd told her, he has a beautiful voice.

They wanted to be there not to jeer but to *cheer*.

On a random Friday afternoon, the kid who had bullied my son reminded me once again of what's true of every single one of us: there is a light beneath our darkness—an instinct to love, a compulsion to care, a heart of humility, an appreciation of beauty, an attraction to that which is good and sacred. Dig for that light and eventually you'll find it. Every single time.

When I was three years old, my family began attending a small evangelical church in rural Illinois. In many ways, the faith tradition of my childhood shaped me well. It scared me enough to keep me out of trouble. It gave me a bit of certainty in a chaotic world. And it gave me a reason to care about other people. But in the long run, it stopped shaping me well—the fear eventually became shame, the certainty fed my ego, and caring for people morphed into an agenda for people.

Somewhere along the way, I began to lose faith in the faith of my childhood. It crumbled a little bit in young adulthood when I discovered an author named Philip Yancey. His writing made space for doubt in the midst of all my certainty. It crumbled even more when I came across the writings of a contemplative priest named Henri Nouwen, whose books helped me to exchange certainty for mystery and agendas for sincere compassion. All that remained was my shame and fear about who I was underneath the surface of me.

That fear crumbled almost completely during my first decade as a psychologist.

The worldview in which I was raised had taught me that human beings are all basically bad to the bone and sinful to the center. Thus, I assumed my job as a therapist was to help people get to the ugliness at the bottom of themselves, so they could figure out what to do with it. But every time—*every time*—as we dug through the ugliness, we found beauty at the bottom instead. Without exception, going deep with my clients ended not with unmitigated darkness, but with the discovery of an inalterable, holy light.

A dazzling *spark*.

My childhood faith died slowly, but the dying was okay, even necessary, because a thing has to die before it can be resurrected. A faith of fear and shame and certainty and ego and agenda had to pass away in order for a faith of trust and mystery and compassion and communion to be resurrected. Death and resurrection. It's been the rhythm of my faith, and it is the rhythm I now see in the world around me—in a world that dies in winter and is resurrected in a flurry of springtime; in forests that burn down and then burst up fragile and green out of the gray ashes; in old ways of seeing ourselves that must die so a new vision of who we are can come to life.

When I reflect back now on the faith of my youth, I don't necessarily consider it a wrong way to see people so much as a *shallow* way. And I don't mean shallow as in conceited or ignorant or vapid. I mean shallow as in not deep enough. When we dare to look beneath the surface of our lives, we can't stop at the the darkness that hides just underneath our carefully crafted facades. We have to keep looking.

For what's *underneath* our underneath.

About a month after Aidan's talent show, as summer break approached, my first-grade son, Quinn, brought home all of his reading projects from the school year. Nestled among them was a handmade card, created for him by his fifth-grade reading buddy—a mentor who had worked with him weekly on his reading. Throughout the year, Quinn had mentioned his reading buddy on several occasions, always smiling about their time together. I opened the card to find out what this lovely fifth grader, who made my son's year such a joy, had said to him in parting. Once again, I was stopped short.

Quinn's reading buddy was Aidan's bully.

In the card, he'd written words of encouragement to Quinn, telling him how much he enjoyed their time together. And then I read something that took a wrecking ball to whatever remained of my childhood religious pessimism about what exists at the bottom of the human heart. In eleven-year-old print, he'd written: "You're already a better reader than I am!"

From bully to buddy. From darkness to light.

Dig deep. Wait for it. And eventually the light splits you open. Every time.

One night, my friend heard retching coming from his toddler's bedroom. He entered the room to find his son, still asleep, covered in his own vomit. He immediately decided his son was ruined. He saw the layer of puke and decided there couldn't possibly be anything good remaining underneath the mess. So my friend left his son lying there and went back to sleep.

Actually . . .

As you might imagine, he did quite the opposite. His heart broke with compassion for his little one. He went directly to him and picked him up, covering himself in the sick mess too. He took his son to the bathtub, drew some warm water, and gently wiped him clean until the pristine boy underneath could be seen once again. He did what loving parents do: he remembered and restored the beauty underneath the mess.

These days, when I go to church and the prayers include words like "Our Father who art in heaven," I no longer think of a deity who is disappointed in my facade and disgusted with what lies just underneath it. I think instead of my friend, overcome with compassion, wiping away his son's vomit. These days, when I've made a mess of things and sense God standing in the doorway, I know he sees what is pristine underneath my puke. I know he sees the beauty beneath the mess, and he just wants to wash the mess away. Because he knows even better than I do:

Our darkness can't withstand our light,

if we insist upon digging deep,

into the bright abyss underneath our underneath.

— CHAPTER 6 —

The First Breadcrumb on the Way to Your Worthiness

What do you do with the mad that you feel?

MISTER ROGERS

*H*ave you ever noticed some children's stories aren't very . . . childlike? In the fairy tale *Hansel and Gretel*, there's a famine, a wicked stepmother, and a plan to lead two little ones into the woods to abandon them there. Fewer mouths to feed.

Yikes.

At any rate, the little ones get wind of the plan and Hansel gets ready by collecting white pebbles. As the children are led into the forest, he drops the pebbles along the way—obvious landmarks by which they find their way home. Foiled, the wicked stepmother tries again. And again, Hansel foils her plan with his little white stones. Not to be fooled three times, she locks the children away so they can't collect rocks. Hansel does the best he can—he grabs a piece of bread and, as they are led into the forest once again, he makes a trail of breadcrumbs. The problem with breadcrumbs, though, is that they can be eaten, blown away, brushed aside, and are difficult to see in the dark. Consequently, Hansel and Gretel get lost in the forest, stumbling upon a witch's gingerbread house.

We're all a bit like Hansel and Gretel. We find ourselves wandering in a dark wood called shame, and we have a trail of breadcrumbs that might lead us back to who we really are, but it's hard to find the first breadcrumb in all the darkness. It's hard to find it because, at first, it looks like it's *part* of our darkness. Maybe I can shine a little light on it though.

The first breadcrumb is our anger.

"You must be so full of rage."

I was sitting in a pub with a friend. We were not yet close friends, but I had come to trust his wisdom in matters of the psyche, so I'd invited him to dinner, hoping he would give me some practical tips about how to handle a situation in my life.

Instead, with one sentence, he changed my life.

I had told him about a scene I recently witnessed in which Aidan, who was seven years old at the time, carried on a more-mature-than-normal conversation with an adult, asking the big person question after question about the big person's life. I watched and wondered if the big person would reciprocate and demonstrate an interest in Aidan. Eventually, it happened—the big person asked Aidan a question about himself. But when Aidan began to talk about his week, I watched the eyes of the big person become glassy, gazing off into the distance. Aidan quickly noticed, stopped mid-sentence, got up, and went to find something else to do. I watched as he learned a little lesson about not being interesting enough. Something deep inside of me ached.

And seethed.

I told my friend I'd felt an almost violent urge to protect Aidan from what happened. My friend listened and then told me the thing that changed my life. He told me I must be full of anger about my *own* experience of glassy eyes and distant gazes. He told me I must be enraged by my *own* little lessons in not being interesting enough. And he told me I needed to go toward the anger to see where it would lead me. Like a breadcrumb, marking a trail out of the wilderness.

I looked at him quizzically.

Anger was not an emotion with which I identified, so it was with utter sincerity that I replied, "Nope. No anger. Just not sure how to handle the situation if it happens again." My friend had the wisdom to let it go, but at the end of the conversation, he gave me the name of a therapist. I smiled and said thank you, but really I was thinking to myself, *How silly. I'm fine.* Yet, like I said, I trusted him in matters of the psyche.

So I started watching for breadcrumbs.

Over the next week, I began to notice the many small and not-so-small ways my anger was leaking out all over the people in my life. I barked at my kids for being kids. I criticized my wife for not being me. I was unreasonably annoyed at the cashier who didn't make eye contact. I smashed my fist against the steering wheel when another driver acted like I didn't exist. Then one afternoon, I almost snapped at the parent of a therapy client when she refused to be interested in the suffering of her child. Finally, I had to admit to myself that maybe, just maybe, I might possibly need a little help, because I just might have a little anger problem. Maybe. Possibly.

It turns out I do. It turns out we all do.

Most of us don't know what to do with our anger. Some of us try to put a lid on it, afraid of what we might be capable of if our anger isn't contained. Yet human beings are cracked and dripping vessels, and our anger inevitably leaks out. We do and say things we don't want to do and say. We end up taking our anger out on others, then we regret what we've done and take it out on ourselves.

Others of us have become so skilled at burying our anger we don't even know it's there. While this strategy tends to appear healthier, it has significant consequences for our long-term well-being. Suppressing anger requires an enormous amount of psychic effort—it saps our energy and drains our emotional resources, resulting in fatigue at best and depression at worst. In other words, sometimes depression is an emotional state in and of itself, but just as often, depression is a state of emotional fatigue resulting from the enormous effort required to suppress one of our most potent emotions: anger.

Finally, there are those of us who have quit trying to contain our anger altogether and have flung wide the doors of rage. A few minutes on Facebook is enough to see that some of us have made anger our preferred way of relating to the world. And we do great damage with it. We rage on the roads and in our homes. We flood our lives with resentment, one furious day at a time.

Whether we tend to suppress anger or give it free rein, it has devastating consequences. Yet the worst consequence is not what we do to ourselves when we bury it, or what we do to others when we don't; it's what we don't allow it to do *for* us. When we deny or indulge our anger, we don't give it a chance to be a breadcrumb. We don't let it lead us back home through the wilderness of our shame and to the warm hearth of our worthiness. So the real question is not "Do you get mad?" The real question, in the words of the beloved Mister Rogers, is this: "What do you do with the mad that you feel?"

When I was young, I often felt very confused by the contradictions in Scripture. For instance, in one scene, Jesus—a teacher of peace, love, and forgiveness—becomes openly angry. He makes a whip out of cords, enters the temple in Jerusalem, and drives out the money traders and sellers by toppling their furniture. As a kid, I had no idea what to do with this story. I couldn't reconcile the paradoxical images of the gentle teacher and the angry reformer—so I mentally discarded it, as we so often do with the parts of life and faith that don't easily make sense. Now, though, I believe the story harbors an essential truth about how the human heart is healed.

Corruption had invaded the heart of the temple, and it seems the first step in restoring the sacredness of that holy space was a focused anger, intended to drive the corruption out. Interestingly, these same Scriptures later introduce the radically new idea that human beings—not buildings—are the temples in which God has chosen to dwell. So, maybe when corruption—when *shame*—enters into the heart of a *human being*, the appropriate and holy response is anger as well. Maybe when shame gets all the way to the center of us, anger is an important part of chasing it back out again.

Your heart is a temple—the dwelling place of God. As such, it is holy and wholly good. Yet shame is being bought, sold, and traded at the center of you. It distorts the good heart you have, uses it for its own profit, and cheapens the sacred space within you. What if your anger includes the holy impulse to run shame right out of you and to restore the temple of your heart to its intended condition?

I called the therapist, and I did the therapy. For about a year. And a year as a therapy client taught me far more than a decade as a therapist ever could. It taught me this: anger isn't an inherently bad thing.

Anger becomes a *destructive* thing when we allow it to become a *reactive* thing instead of harnessing it as a *guiding* thing. In other words, anger is the first breadcrumb on the path back to ourselves, so if we deny it—if we kick the breadcrumb into the underbrush—we lose our way. If we throw that breadcrumb at everyone else, we wound them, and we still lose our way. But if we pick up that breadcrumb, attend to it, turn it over in our hands and in our hearts, appreciate it for what it is and what it has to teach us, then we can look for the next breadcrumb on the path leading back to our worthiness.

In the years since my year of therapy, everything about the therapy I practice with my clients has changed. Before, I often struggled with where to begin the process of healing shame. Now I know, every time, we begin by finding the first breadcrumb. We have to find the anger. Sometimes, when it's been buried deep, that's hard to do. Other times, of course, it's very easy to do.

But whether the finding is difficult or easy, it's always the beginning. And that's good news. Because the trail of breadcrumbs ultimately leads us beneath our first-layer facade and through the layer of darkness underneath, to what's underneath our underneath. It is the trail that leads to the light. And there we find, lonely and waiting, the little one who has been standing all the while at the intersection of our worthiness and our shame.

When your anger leaks out, how old do you feel? Better yet, how old do you *act*? Because there is a little one inside of you who is precisely that age—a little one who was present as your sense of worthiness began to diminish and your shame began to grow. When you follow your anger back to its source, you will find the little one inside of you who has been furiously protecting your enough-ness all along. And that kid has every right to be a little angry.

As you get reacquainted with that little one, you will also get reacquainted with the worthiness that has been preserved somewhere near the center of you. You will become grateful to him or her for holding on to the sense of worthiness you thought you'd lost. Then you will relieve the little one of this burden. You'll say, "Rest now, little one, I can take it from here." And that will be another beginning.

It will be the beginning of trading in your anger for tenderness.

You see, anger is a bottomless resource—it can't be reduced by expressing it. Anger begets anger. Anger feeds on itself. But anger can be exchanged. It can be traded in for the next breadcrumb, which is usually fear. And then your fear will lead you to your sorrow and sadness and grief. But the good news is that sorrow, sadness, and grief *do* diminish when they are expressed, and something else begins to grow in their place: joy, lightness, tenderness, and, eventually and blessedly, forgiveness. Forgiveness of glassy eyes and distant gazes. Forgiveness, even, of those who led you into your dark wood.

But you can't rush it, friend. The restoration of your heart can only happen one breadcrumb at a time. Start by looking for your anger, and let it lead you back to everything that is loveable within you. Let it lead you home.

CHAPTER 7

Why the Secret to Being Worthy Is Doing Nothing

*People may spend their whole lives climbing the
ladder of success only to find, once they reach the top,
that the ladder is leaning against the wrong wall.*

THOMAS MERTON

*I*n my earliest memory, I was not caught red-handed; I was caught red-*toothed.*

I remember a summer morning when I was five years old. I don't remember sliding out of bed early while the household slumbered. I don't remember opening the refrigerator door. I don't remember drinking the cherry Kool-Aid. I don't remember how sweet it tasted. My memory begins with my father standing over me.

I remember him asking if I had anything to tell him. I remember saying no. I remember my heart beating a little more quickly than usual. And then my memory fades again. I don't remember what happened next. It's possible my father handled it perfectly. It's possible he didn't. I only remember how I felt when it was all said and done: I had *done* something bad, so I felt like I *was* something bad. In other words, I felt shame.

I don't remember a time in my life when I didn't feel this way.

Many of us don't. Because often, it is the trauma of shame that shocks us into conscious awareness of our self—it makes us, literally, self-conscious. So, our first memory of who we are is usually of our darkness tangled up with feelings of confusion and embarrassment. We rarely remember the precious months or years when we experienced our worthiness as a fact. A given. Something as present, real, and natural as breathing and playing and animal crackers. We have amnesia for the good thing we instinctively knew ourselves to be before shame startled us into self-consciousness.

We can't remember our light.

After the morning of the red teeth, my memory fades again and then resumes several months later. I'm standing in the same living room, but this time, instead of holding my shame in, I'm holding a soccer trophy up. This time, my memory begins with a gold trophy, naming me the most improved player on the team. My father and my family are looking at me and approving of me and admiring me. I'm feeling worthy. And I'm beginning to believe something: my gold trophies might be the solution to my red teeth—I may be bad but I can do good things, and if I do enough good things, maybe, just maybe, I'll be good enough.

Red teeth and gold trophies.

Our lives are a pendulum swinging between shame and worthiness.

This is being human.

What I do is who I am.

It's a lesson we learn at an early age. Sometimes we learn it painfully, when our mistakes are met with red rage and burning words or icy stares and even colder silence. Other times we learn it intellectually, when we're taught we are only as worthy as our most disappointing losses, only as strong as our weakest moments, and only as successful as our most public failures. Most of the time, though, we learn it *accidentally*.

Do you remember?

Do you remember how the people you loved seemed to love you a little more when you said the right thing or did the thing they wished you to do? Do you remember how they seemed to like you a little less after the temper tantrum in the grocery store or after you spilled the grape juice on the new carpet? Quietly and subtly, our sense of worth gets fused with our actions. And then all of life reinforces these accidental lessons in shame: our friends and teachers and report cards and spouses and bosses and job reviews confirm what we've begun to suspect—we're only as valuable as the valuable things we do.

Do you remember your red teeth and your gold trophies?

Thomas Merton observed, "People may spend their whole lives climbing the ladder of success only to find, once they reach the top, that the ladder is leaning against the wrong wall." If we aren't careful, we can spend our whole lives climbing, believing we are what we do and what we do has the power to make us worthy. We can get addicted to the high of transient self-esteem that comes with achieving each new rung, and then, as the rush of each success fades, we start craving the next rung and the next high. When our doing doesn't do away with our shame, we start doing *more*. And then we end up frustrated, fatigued, frayed, and feeling like a failure. The ladder of success, it turns out, is leaning against the wall of our shame.

What red teeth are you running from, and what gold trophies are you running for? What if, instead of running for trophies, you decided to run back to your true self—to the forgotten little one inside of you who has been holding on to your sense of worthiness all along? And what if, along the way, you discovered your true self is not something you have to *run* to, but something you get to *settle* into?

Last spring, I coached my son's kindergarten soccer team. They were unusually talented kids, so they scored a lot of goals. After each goal, all five faces on the field would turn to look at me, smiles as wide as the goalposts. I would meet their smiles with my own, and then I would meet them at midfield to celebrate with high fives all around.

Then, last autumn, I coached my son's first-grade soccer team. They were really good kids too, but they weren't nearly as skilled. When a goal was scored, it was usually scored against us. After each goal, the faces of my players would still turn to look at me, though they weren't filled with smiles; they were filled with a question: *Will you still meet us at midfield with a high five?*

In those moments, before I could answer the question on their faces, I first had to answer to the pit in my stomach. The pit in my stomach tells me life is about winning and losing, success and failure, what we achieve and what we don't. It thinks we're crazy to give a trophy to every kid on a soccer field because it sends the message that all the kids performed equally and admirably. It wonders how our kids will even survive in a competitive world if they haven't been taught the hierarchy of success. The pit in my stomach wants to tell the kids what they did wrong so it won't happen again. It wants to make them look at their red teeth.

Yet, I know the pit in my stomach is really an echo of the shame in my heart. And I want something better for these kids—I don't want them to spend their lives compulsively chasing gold trophies to compensate for their red teeth, as I have done. Whenever we arrive at a place of wanting something better for the people we love, we can be sure we have arrived at the place of our own wounding—the desire to prevent pain for the ones we love always arises from an empathy embedded in our own painful experiences. The wounded kid in me knows these little faces aren't asking me how to win.

They're asking if they are still *enough.*

So when the other team scored against us, I sprinted for midfield. I was waiting for my team when they arrived, and I gave high fives all around, as if *we* had scored the goal. Because when a bunch of six-year-olds fail and then look to you, they're never wondering how they *did*; they're always wondering who they *are*. They're not wondering who gets the biggest trophy; they're wondering who gets the biggest hug.

Don't we all still have the upturned face of a six-year-old inside of us? And isn't that child still asking the same kinds of questions? *Am I worthy, even in the midst of my failures? Am I enough, even when I'm a mess? Will you meet me at midfield, even when I'm losing at life?*

A couple of years ago, while cleaning out the garage on an autumn afternoon, I came across three boxes of my childhood trophies. I had moved eight times since earning the last of those trophies, and I thought I'd disposed of all my childhood belongings in the process. But these had survived every move.

We don't relinquish our worthiness projects easily, do we?

I pulled out the trophies one at a time, reminiscing about the battles won and lost, the rungs reached and the rungs I couldn't reach. It was a tender moment, but it was also bittersweet. Those trophies didn't just represent the ladder I had climbed; they were also a reminder of the ladder I was *still* climbing. They were icons of a life focused on doing things to become a worthy thing. Yet, on that autumn afternoon, I wanted to be done reaching for rungs.

I wanted to meet myself at midfield instead.

I imagined the upturned face of the six-year-old kid inside of me, asking, *Am I worthy even when I fail?* I wanted to meet that little guy with a high five. And then I wanted to take him by the shoulders, look him in the eye, and tell him he isn't his successes or his failures, his mistakes or his good fortune, his hard work or his apathy, his lucky guesses or his bad decisions, his red teeth or his gold trophies. I wanted to tell him to go brush his red teeth and then come back to midfield for another high five.

And a hug.

On an autumn afternoon, I decided I was done trying to hide my red teeth with my gold trophies, done trying to climb out of my shame with honors and accomplishments and success. I decided it was time to become still again, to stop trying to become something else and to start letting myself be the someone I already am, to settle into the mystery of what I'd forgotten. So, one by one, I placed each trophy in the garbage can, and I made a little more space in my life.

Space for my light to shine through.

The first act of our story is often a challenging one. But the challenge is usually the opposite of what we assume it to be. During our backstory, we arduously cobble together the best self we can—an amalgam of relationships and accomplishments, approval and awards—because we've been led to believe the original self that was put together *for* us—our true self, our loveable self—is not enough. Our first act, though, is not about more cobbling; in fact, it's about halting the construction project altogether, and probably even deconstructing a bit of what we've put together.

In our first act, we don't ultimately become who we are; we *un*become who we are *not*.

Our first act is not about climbing higher on the ladder of success; it's about stepping down. It's about letting go of the things we do to feel worthy, so we can return to who we were before we forgot. We don't need a ladder to construct who we are supposed to be; we need an oxygen mask to resuscitate who we've always been. We don't need to build; we simply need to breathe.

Our breath, it turns out, is one of the best tools we have.

When you breathe, you are not building a breathtaking life; you are simply taking the breath that gives you life. You are not moving up; you are settling down. You are not trying to win a trophy; you are simply being you.

Can you sense what a great act of faith this is? To stop all of your doing and to simply breathe, even for ten minutes, when you still believe your doing is what makes you worthy? To quit performing while you're still wondering if your performance has been acceptable? There's no to-do list for this kind of moment, because there is literally nothing to do. In fact, the task is to slowly settle into *doing* nothing so you can experience *being* something, even while that something remains a mystery to you. And it requires only one thing: you have to dare to believe the something you are is alight with worthiness.

So, for now, just breathe. Let the air run through your teeth.

No matter how red they are.

CHAPTER 8

The Difference Between Getting Rich and Living Richly

Each human being has a place of poverty . . .
Let's dare to see our poverty as the land
where our treasure is hidden.

HENRI NOUWEN

I was born to a drug dealer and his quiet wife.

When I was two, he was caught in the act and incarcerated, and by the time I saw him again, he had become a Christian. I was too young to remember any of it, but a lot changed after that. That's when we started going to church on the weekends and, a little later, my parents started going to college during the week—my dad studying psychology and my mom studying nursing. Two tuition payments plus three children equaled eight years of scarcity. By the time I was in third grade, we were scraping by in a mobile home, with my mother working as a nurse at night and my father going to school during the day. What they did was heroic.

Sometimes, heroism is not very glamorous.

We had a television that broadcast mostly static, a car that couldn't make right turns, and the constant trailer park fear of tornadoes. We had fights about grocery money. We had fights about *every* kind of money. We had a claustrophobic hallway that ended at a claustrophobic bedroom I shared with my brother. We had a basketball hoop down the street—an old rusted rim tied to a telephone pole with yellow twine. No backboard. No net. We had bullies who chased me home from the basketball court.

I usually got away.

We had a tiny bathroom in our trailer with a tiny bathtub. Sometimes we had hot water. Sometimes we didn't. One night, when the hot water ran out, my dad ran out of patience. My mom was at work, and Dad said he was leaving too. He tried, but I wrapped myself around his leg and wouldn't let go. He stayed.

But my shame stayed too.

I had a friend who didn't live in the trailer park. His dad was a doctor, and their car could turn in both directions. His TV had options, and his house was attached to the ground. His basketball hoop had a garage behind it, and his bathtub had water at whatever temperature you wanted. He had boxes full of G.I. Joe action figures, and we played with them on a lawn made of grass instead of dust. His yard had a fence that kept the bullies out. And his parents didn't look like they were on the verge of leaving anytime soon. They were affluent and they seemed happy, and when I was with them, for some reason, I felt a little less alone, a little less ashamed.

So, at some point, I decided making money could make me worthy.

Shame comes and goes and it's hard to put a finger on the exact moment of its birth. But once it is born, it almost always grows into the same conclusion: I'm not *filled* with worthiness, so I will try to *surround* myself with it. I may not *be* a valuable thing, but I can *purchase* valuable things.

When you doubt the quality of your heart, you increase the quantity of your stuff. You tell yourself the next gadget will make everything better. Or the next house. Or the next investment. And before long, you've confused your net worth with the worth of your soul.

On a Sunday morning, a quarter of a century after leaving the trailer park, I wake up feeling, once again, like I'm not worth very much. Overnight, my shame has resurfaced. I'm tempted to speculate about why—like an alcoholic trying to identify the trigger for his relapse—but I don't. It's what shame does. It hibernates and then it wakes up. And it doesn't keep a schedule.

Around midmorning, we go to church. There, I can usually find my way back to the spark at the center of me. Sometimes it's the *place* that helps—the socializing and the songs and the sermon that silence the voice of shame within me; but other times it's just the *space*—the space to be still and listen for a kinder voice inside of me. On this morning, though, the place and the space make me feel even lonelier. So I put on a smile that isn't real, sing songs that ring hollow, and harbor doubts it seems no one else is harboring. Then I go home and scour the newspaper for sales on electronics. The iPad mini catches my eye. I know exactly what I'm doing. And I don't care.

I get in the car and head for the mall.

As the Apple store comes into view, I see it's overflowing with people. I enter my name into a long queue. And I wait. The employees are hustling, but they can't keep up with demand. When my turn finally comes, I ask the salesperson why it's so busy on a Sunday afternoon. He looks at me with a wry smile and says, "This is *quiet*."

As he finalizes my purchase, I stand back and watch the faces in the crowd around me. I see anger and frustration. I see anxiety. I see sadness. I see blank stares. In an Apple store, I see the many masks of our shame—I witness the many guises of our inner poverty—and I watch us try to buy our way out of it. Then I do it too. And it works. For a little while. But the problem with retail therapy is that it doesn't *heal* our shame. It *mutes* it.

Temporarily.

Shame gets submerged beneath the stuff we buy, but there in the depths it continues to fester and multiply. Our material possessions increase, but our inner poverty does too. Author and philosopher Henry David Thoreau wrote, "The mass of men lead lives of quiet desperation." What is a life of quiet desperation? It's trying to buy your way into a sense of worthiness and then, as the rush of each purchase subsides, feeling the shame resurface, because a credit card can't heal a heart.

Quiet desperation is not knowing what else to do.

On a lazy Labor Day afternoon, almost three decades after moving out of the mobile home, I stumble across a little bit of actual healing. I'm in my basement instead of an Apple store, and I'm holding an old children's book instead of an iPad.

Something besides my trophies did survive all my moves.

Thirty years earlier, my father had completed his bachelor's degree in the town with the trailer park, and we had subsequently returned to my hometown in Illinois. The book had been given to me on the eve of moving away, as a farewell gift from the parents of my friend with the fence and the lawn made of grass instead of dust. I hadn't thought of the book in years, but on this particular afternoon, as I'd been contemplating moving my own family back to that same hometown, I'd had a vague memory of an inscription on the inside cover of the book.

So now I'm holding this book called *Rascal*. The dust jacket is long gone. The corners are frayed and the pages are brittle, but when I lift the front cover, I see faded blue ink on the first blank, yellowing page. In script clearly written with great care, my friend's mother had written these words: "To Kelly, who is anything but a rascal . . . May you grow in the grace and knowledge of the Lord." It was signed and dated May 1986.

I was nine.

For thirty years, I had attributed my warm memories of their family to the stuff they had, and then chased after the same kind of stuff for myself. On this Labor Day afternoon, though, I realize I've gotten it all wrong. I don't remember them warmly because of their good stuff; I remember them warmly because of the good stuff they saw in *me*. I remember them warmly because they saw underneath my underneath. I remember them warmly because they gave me—the poor kid from the other side of the tracks—a chance to see my true self reflected in their eyes. I remember them because the little one who clung to his father's leg, terrified of being abandoned, needed desperately to be assured he wasn't a rascal—he needed to know he was loveable.

I remember them because they were grace to me.

Years ago, these good people wrote these good words about me and *for* me, and the words sat neglected and mostly forgotten in a box all that time. I think that's how our hearts work too. People write good things on them, but until we're ready to read and receive those graceful words, we close up our heart like a book and pack it away. Instead of opening up the front cover of who we are to find the little bit of love that has been inscribed on us, we open up our wallets and try to find worthiness another way.

Perhaps it's time we put away our wallets and dig our hearts out of the box. Perhaps it's time to open them up and read the good words people have written there. Perhaps it's time we dare to believe that the people who have loved us well—even if briefly and fleetingly—have seen us more accurately than we've seen ourselves. Perhaps it's time to believe the teacher or the coach or the parent or the pastor or the boyfriend or the girlfriend or the husband or the wife actually knew what they were talking about. Perhaps then we'd know: life isn't about getting rich; it's about living *richly.*

Getting rich is about the size of your wallet; living richly is about the size of your heart. Getting rich is about how you number your houses; living richly is about how you number your days. Getting rich is about ending up with a pile of stuff; living richly is about remembering we all end up in a pile of dust. Getting rich is about attracting the right kind of people; living richly is about being attracted to *all* kinds of people. Getting rich is about accumulating shiny things; living richly is about trusting you have the strength to face terrible things. Getting rich is about moving up; living richly is about getting knocked down and believing in yourself enough to get up again.

But most importantly, getting rich is so often about avoiding our inner poverty—the sad, scared, shaming voices within—while living richly is about choosing to embrace it. You're a human being, so you have this kind of poverty within you. You can choose to pursue upward mobility, which mutes those voices temporarily, like I did. Or you can choose to pursue *inward* mobility, which means venturing inside of yourself to become familiar with your sadness, fear, and shame. Eventually, I did that too. And I can assure you, when you really pay attention to them—when you really listen—they begin, gradually, to quiet down. Then, in this rich new interior silence, you can start listening for the voices who have, all along, been calling you worthy.

Or at least not a rascal.

— CHAPTER 9 —

Why We Need to Quit Looking into Mirrors
(and Become a Mirror)

*There is a secret relationship between
our physical being and the rhythm of our soul.
The body is the place where the soul shows itself.*

JOHN O'DONOHUE

*C*an you guess what the most popular tourist attraction in Chicago
is? It isn't the Willis Tower—formerly the Sears Tower—one
of the tallest buildings in the United States, from which you can
see for miles across urban canyons of steel. It isn't Navy Pier, where
you can ride a Ferris wheel while viewing both the vastness of Lake
Michigan and of the Chicago skyline. And it isn't Chicago's world-
renowned architectural tour, during which you travel the Chicago
River by boat and learn how the city resurrected itself from the
ashes of the Great Chicago Fire.

No, the most popular attraction in Chicago is . . . wait for it . . .
a *bean*.

More precisely, it's a sculpture called *Cloud Gate*. Measuring
sixty-six feet long and forty-two feet high, the bean is crafted from

168 seamless, stainless steel, mirror-like plates and shaped like a bean with an arched underbelly that allows pedestrians to walk beneath it. The exterior of the sculpture reflects the city's magnificent skyline, but invariably you will find visitors crowded under the arch, captivated by their various reflections, mirrored from every direction by the rounded surface of the bean. Why is this giant metal bean so popular?

Because we human beings can't get enough of our mirrors.

We were teenage boys and we were surrounded by mirrors.

My hometown in rural Illinois is a good town—the kind of good only a small town can be. My small town had a small YMCA with a small weight room. And the walls of the weight room were covered with mirrors.

Have you ever watched a bunch of adolescent boys dripping with sweat, hormones, and insecurity lift weights in a crowd of their peers—and a crowd of mirrors? It's quite a sight. The boldest of us performed our lifts and then stood before the mirrors, twitching and flexing, judging our bodies from every angle. The rest of us pretended we were too cool for our own reflections. Meanwhile, we snuck sideways glances at ourselves, clandestinely evaluating our size and shape and firmness. No matter what, I couldn't get my pecs to bounce. But I kept lifting and looking sideways anyway.

Back then, young men had to go to the weight room to look in the mirror, but young women carried mirrors everywhere, so they could see their reflection whenever they wanted. Now, however, we all carry a digital mirror with us wherever we go—our smartphones. With the tap of an icon, the camera view is reversed and our digital image can be captured forever—the selfie is our newest kind of mirror. Why are we so preoccupied with mirrors?

Because we were made for mirrors.

At the conclusion of Marc Webb's film *The Amazing Spider-Man*, Peter Parker's English teacher declares, "There is only one plot in all of fiction: Who am I?" She's almost right. It may not be the *only* plot in all of fiction, but it is the *foundational* plot in all of fiction. It is the engine driving every story, and in the story of our lives, it is the question around which our first act revolves. *Who am I? And is who I am good enough?*

As children, our whole lives are a question asked: *Will you be my mirror? Will you see me deeply enough, and abide with me steadily enough, to reflect back to me who I am and who I am becoming?* If we are seen and mirrored well by the people we love, our life ceases to be a question asked and becomes an answer lived. *If* we are mirrored well.

The problem is, most of our mirrors—the people who could have reflected our hearts back to us—were cracked. Those we looked to for mirroring were, for the most part, not *bad* people; they were *broken* people. In other words, they were normal people. Still preoccupied with their own inner drama, they were too busy asking *Who am I?* to answer that question for us. Still absorbed with their own search for worthiness, they were too distracted to mirror the worthiness in us. Still in search of their own mirror, they may have even used us as a mirror for themselves. Or, still cracked by their own shame, they may have cracked us a little bit too. Thus, as we grew bigger, so did the need for an answer to our question: *Who am I?*

If we can't find anyone to adequately mirror our heart, we'll settle for any kind of mirror we can find. And there is one kind of mirror we do not have to look hard to find: body mirrors. They're *everywhere*. In weight rooms, restrooms, makeup aisles, smartphones, and in giant stainless steel beans.

And, of course, in dressing rooms . . .

On a Saturday afternoon, I'm sitting in my living room when I get a text message from a friend who's sitting outside the women's dressing room in a department store. He's waiting while his wife tries on dresses for an upcoming event. As he waits, he watches a parade of women walk out of changing rooms and stand in front of mirrors, looking themselves over, evaluating their bodies from every angle. He watches face after face fill with disappointment, self-rejection, even self-loathing. There are few exceptions. He tells me these women are ruthless toward themselves. He says it's heartbreaking to watch.

In the absence of heart mirrors, we gaze into body mirrors, searching for the answer to our question of identity, and the shameful message slowly and subtly seeps into us: I am my body. I am my skin, my shape, my measurements, my weight, my firmness, and my youthfulness. I am my body, so I can make myself a better me by changing my appearance and preserving my youth. I can diet and exercise and poke and prod and have surgeries and get injections and buy more products. The numbers on the scale tell me who I am. The people who like or reject my body tell me who I am. The mirrors in the dressing room tell me who I am.

A week later, I'm sitting in the same living room and I get another message. This time, though, it's not from my friend; it's from Caitlin, who is four years old at the time. And it's not a text message; it's a message in flesh and blood. She's been in her room playing quietly for a while, but when she emerges, Caitlin has been replaced by a pirate.

Except not exactly.

Sure, there's the eye patch and the woolen cap with the skull and crossbones and the plastic sword in a hilt at her waist. But there's also a copious amount of costume jewelry. And a dress. And pink, bejeweled sunglasses covering half her face. And she's carrying a baby, not like a pirate would, but like a mother would. She hasn't looked in a mirror and it wouldn't even occur to her to do so, because she isn't yet looking into body mirrors for her identity. She hasn't yet confused her skin with her soul; instead, she lets her skin *express* her soul. By the standards of almost any body mirror, she looks utterly ridiculous.

By the standards of a heart mirror, though, she is utterly beautiful.

I look at her and I know my daughter has expressed her soul perfectly. She's equal parts mischievous pirate, glamorous runway model, and tender mother. So I try to be a not-too-broken heart mirror. I tell her I love all of it, and I ask her to growl like a pirate and strut like a model and show me how to feed the baby. Because I don't want her to try to change her body, and I don't even want her to try to accept it. I want her to simply let it be a manifestation of her heart.

In all its ridiculous beauty.

For decades, we human beings have obsessed about changing our bodies. Now the tide is turning a little bit, and we are talking more about accepting them. Even the personal care brand Dove is sponsoring advertising campaigns about accepting our figures and our faces. But I think the movement to accept our bodies is equally riddled with shame and just as doomed to failure.

Because the mind plays tricks.

You can't think less about something by trying to think about it less. If, for instance, I told you not to think about white bears, all you would think about is white bears. And, similarly, you can't accept something by trying to accept it. Whether you are looking at your body to judge it or accept it, you're still looking at your body. When you try to accept your body by focusing on your body, you are trying to solve the problem by practicing the problem, and the problem is this: if you look to your body to tell you who you are, you'll never get around to looking for your heart. If you're focused on your body image—positively or negatively—you'll never get around to focusing on your *soul* image. If you search for your identity on the surface of yourself, you'll never get around to searching for it underneath, at the center of yourself. So, instead of obsessing about changing your body or accepting your body, what if you let yourself *forget* about your body, for just a little while, like a little girl dressed up as a pirate-supermodel-mother. What if you forgot about your body so you could remember your heart?

It's not easy.

I look in the mirror and I see bald and gray and wrinkling—and my pecs still won't bounce—so it's tempting to make "worn out" and "used up" part of my identity. But what if, instead of looking into mirrors at our surface, we became a mirror for the little kid in our depths—that young child who needs someone to reflect who they are and who they are becoming? What if, instead of trying to *look* good, you spent some time searching for the uncertain little kid within, so you could assure that child he or she *is* good? What if you have a little one inside of you just waiting for a parent to see them and mirror them, and what if *you* could be that parent?

I think you might stop seeing the surface of you as the place where your beauty begins and ends, and you might start to see it as the place where your true beauty *emerges*. Your body is an inevitably aging tableau of fading hair and wrinkling skin and sun spots and sagging spots and endlessly uncooperative pecs, upon which your soul can be innocently and playfully etched. Of course, if you let the little one in the depths of you begin to craft what happens on the surface of you, you might start to look a little more ridiculous.

Ridiculously beautiful.

Like a pirate-supermodel-mother who looks like her true self.

— CHAPTER 10 —

The Good News That Sounds Too Good to Be True

> *When a great moment knocks on the door of your life,*
> *it is very often no louder than the beating of your heart,*
> *and it is very easy to miss it.*
>
> BORIS PASTERNAK

It's another Monday morning, another drive to my daughter's preschool, and, presumably, yet another spin of the *Frozen* soundtrack. Instead, on this morning, Caitlin opens a book and announces she's going to read me a story. She's four—she can't read—but she begins anyway. The story doesn't make much sense, but it's filled with intrigue and love and wounds and forgiveness, and I'm enjoying it immensely when a new character enters the story and, abruptly, Caitlin stops and growls at herself.

"Uuuggghhh," she mutters.

I see her solemn face in the rearview mirror, and I raise my eyebrows in a question. She knows what I'm asking and answers me with this: "I told the wrong name." I'm quiet for a moment and then ask, as gently as I can, "But, sweetie, you can't read. How could you say the wrong name?" And she looks at me like I'm an adult who knows a lot of things but has forgotten the most important ones, and says, "Daddy, I quit listening to my *imagination.*"

As she begins to "read" again, I realize I was wrong about what's happening in the back seat. She's not making it up; she's letting it *out.* She's not deciding who she wants the characters to be; she's listening to who they already are. She's taking dictation from a voice she listens to on the inside, a voice that already knows the name of every character.

And maybe it's that simple.

Maybe, just maybe, the spark of God at the center of you doesn't just glow; it also *speaks.* Unceasingly. Of your worthiness. Maybe the spark of the God-who-is-love is always telling you about the lovely soul you are. To hear this voice of grace is to be loved and to know the name of the character you are in the story you are living. It's the name you were given before all other names.

You are Loveable.

The problem is, somewhere along the way, we stopped listening to this voice of grace. Or rather, we began listening, instead, to the voice of shame. It's the choice we made before we knew there was a choice to make. We chose to quit listening to the voice telling us we're lovely and started listening instead to the voice telling us we're a loser. That's how we forget who we are. But it is also how we *remember* who we are—we don't have to try more strenuously; we simply need to listen more closely . . .

We're still driving to preschool as Caitlin's exasperation is replaced by resolve, and she resumes her reading. The pages turn and the plot thickens until once again she stops herself with a mutter.

I look in the rearview mirror and her eyes meet mine once more. "I stopped listening *again*," she says with frustration. But then, resolutely, her eyes return to the book—she corrects the name and resumes her story. Caitlin listens to her guiding voice within. And then she quits listening. And then she starts listening again. Over and over again.

You, too, have a voice within you, and it knows your name. It sees your hidden, holy heart. It knows exactly who you are, and it is telling you that you are loveable, lovely, and beloved. It speaks the language of worthiness, because it knows no other tongue. Amid the fire of your shame, it comes as a gentle, constant whisper.

And it simply waits for you to start listening again.

But listening again doesn't happen all at once, and it doesn't happen once and for all. It happens in fits and starts. Sometimes, no doubt, you will forget to listen—perhaps for many years or even decades—but you can always begin to listen again. Sometimes you might listen for years and never hear it, like listening for the subliminal track on your favorite heavy metal album. Then one lazy summer afternoon, you play the record again and it finally comes through, and from that day forward, it's hard for you to hear anything else. The still, small voice of your divine spark eventually breaks through the heavy metal bass beat of your shame.

This breaking through? This is your inciting incident.

Remember, in a story, the inciting incident is where the story *really* begins. It's the moment in the first act that propels the character into the second act and the heart of their story. It's the point of no return. The protagonist is changed in some fundamental way, and there is no going back. In the story of our lives, the inciting incident is that moment when the voice of the divine spark comes through. It's the moment the magic happens. It's the moment we open up to the possibility of who we might actually be and the light we might actually contain. It's the moment in my friend's dream when she realized God had been offstage all along, whispering repeatedly, "One less day," and that today was *that day*—the day she'd finally see the worthiness she'd always possessed.

Sometimes this voice breaks through "in a dream, in a vision of the night, when deep sleep falls on people," and sometimes it wells up within us when we're wide awake and staring at a lake. My wife's inciting incident happened in the solitude of a lakeside cabin. She was supposed to be in Guatemala, educating teachers about how to disrupt bullying in the Guatemalan schools. She was terribly overworked, and her outreach to Central America was one of the many balls she was juggling. I was secretly praying some of her balls would drop so she could get some rest.

I swear I didn't steal her passport. But it did go missing, and there was too little time to replace it. The Lord works in mysterious ways indeed.

So, with a clear calendar and no flight to catch, she decided to retreat to a friend's vacant cabin. While there, she slept and cooked and prayed and read the Bible and found herself returning to a particular verse: "He will shelter you with his wings." That verse had always distanced her from God. When she read *shelter*, she felt smothered—words about protection that felt like a message about domination. Yet in the stillness of a quiet cabin, she returned to it again and again, listening. Finally, the voice of the spark broke through—decades transformed by a single day, as she was reassured she was made lovely and was loved tenderly by Love itself.

Before coming home, she had the Hebrew word for "shelter" tattooed on her wrist.

Why did my wife's inciting incident happen on that day? I can't know. Thomas Merton writes that there is "no program for this seeing. It is only given. But the gate of heaven is everywhere." The first act of our story is not about making our inciting incident happen, but about making the *conditions* right for it to happen. At the risk of mixing metaphors and bodily senses, hearing the voice of the divine spark within is like making dinner in a crockpot. You put in all the proper ingredients—stillness, silence, breathing, patience, courage, attentiveness, openness, and faith in possibility and beauty and goodness—and then you let the mixture simmer until you catch the aroma of what is cooking. Until you begin to hear the spark.

Of course, sometimes, at first, it might seem too good to be true.

Which, ironically, is why you can trust it *is* true.

Several years ago, on Christmas morning, I gave myself a gift. (This drives my wife a little crazy, but that's a story for another day.) I had purchased a new set of headphones, wrapped them myself, and placed them under the tree. When I opened them, I knew what I was opening. My eyes didn't grow wide with surprise. I didn't feel euphoric. I simply took them out of the package and started using them.

When you first hear the voice of the spark within you, you probably won't unwrap it and receive it like a gift you've given yourself. Instead, you may pull back a piece of wrapping paper, glimpse the gift inside, and drop the love-package in shock, because it is too surprising. Too much. Too good to be true. When you choose to listen to the whisper of worthiness, your first impulse may not be to accept it. A vast ocean of love will open up inside of you, and it might seem like a mirage.

You may cling, at first, to the desert of your shame.

You may look at your darkness and decide it's too black for there to be any light underneath it. You may look at your mess and believe you are too broken to be beloved. Or, on the other hand, it's possible it will feel so good that you will feel *guilty*—it might feel wrong to feel so worthy. You might think yourself cocky and arrogant. In other words, at first, the gift you've opened may not feel like a gift at all.

That's *okay*.

This is a necessary experience, because it is the beginning of your ability to trust that the voice is *in* you but *not* you. It's how you know you're not just giving yourself what you've always wanted to be given, not just telling yourself what you've always wanted to hear. Of course, as you become aware this voice is not your own, you'll wonder where it came from.

Don't. Please don't.

At first, put that question aside. You don't ultimately receive a gift by figuring out who it is from; you receive it by opening it up. So for now, just open slowly, steadily. Just *receive*. The great theologian Paul Tillich described this experience as well as anyone when he wrote:

A wave of light breaks into our darkness, and it is as though a voice were saying, "You are accepted. You are accepted, accepted by that which is greater than you, and the name of which you do not know. Do not ask for the name now; perhaps you will find it later. Do not try to do anything now; perhaps later you will do much. Do not seek for anything, do not perform anything, do not intend anything. Simply accept the fact that you are accepted." If that happens to us, we experience grace.

The spark at the center of you is Grace itself. And it is speaking. It always has been. It is whispering and waiting for you to start listening again. Are you ready to get quiet, to breathe, to go inward, to listen your way through your dark and into your light? Are you ready to receive the gift? Are you ready to hear the good news about who you are? Are you ready to be called Loveable?

Your inciting incident awaits.

CHAPTER 11

What Grace Sees Underneath Your Mess

> *And Grace calls out, "You are not just a disillusioned old man who may die soon, a middle-aged woman stuck in a job and desperately wanting to get out, a young person feeling the fire in the belly begin to grow cold. You may be insecure, inadequate, mistaken, or potbellied. Death, panic, depression, and disillusionment may be near you. But you are not just that. You are accepted." Never confuse your perception of yourself with the mystery that you really are accepted.*
>
> BRENNAN MANNING

I'm wearing a cheap long-haired wig, leather pants, and women's boots with stiletto heels, and I'm walking into my son's elementary school fundraiser, which is being hosted at a posh local country club. A costume contest for parents had been advertised, so earlier in the day, I had walked into a Goodwill store as a suburban dad and walked out as a rock star circa 1985. Now it's 6:00 p.m. and I'm skittering across the icy parking lot toward the ballroom entrance. In four-inch heels.

With my chest hair showing.

As I work to stay upright, I glance around at the rest of the crowd slip-sliding from the parking lot to the entrance. I see lots of ball gowns. And lots of sport coats. I'm trying not to hit the pavement when the realization hits *me*: no one else has chosen to compete. With the exception of the few friends who came with me, everyone else is dressed normally. Classy. Mature.

Somewhere inside of me, the shame of a kid who changed schools three times by fourth grade and always felt a little bit on the outside begins to speak up. The voice of shame in me says: *Everyone else knows what they're doing and you don't. You look silly. Ridiculous. You're a joke.* It evokes memories of loneliness and inadequacy, and it makes proclamations about my unworthiness: *You're not cool enough. You're not popular enough.*

You are, quite simply, not good enough.

The voice of shame within us is crafty, not necessarily because it is saying *bad* things about us, but because it is saying *partial* things about us. Sometimes, it uses half-truths that are hard to argue with and dresses them up as the whole truth—it speaks of the very real, very unpleasant stuff inside of us as if it's the *only* stuff inside of us. Of course we've made mistakes. This is being human. Sometimes we do the best we can and life still ends up a wreck. This is having some skin in the game. Sometimes we'll do almost anything to survive. This is being a part of the big circle of life. Sometimes we know exactly how to do the most loving thing and we choose to do far less. This is having freedom, and fallibility. We're a mess. Of course we are. We have a layer of darkness. Of course we do.

The problem is, when we hear the voice of shame within us, telling us this part-truth about the darkness within us, we try to talk it out of its conclusion. We try to convince ourselves it's wrong and we're not so full of darkness, not such a mess. Sometimes, this tactic might even work—we might silence the voice of shame long enough to get a decent night's sleep, but by morning, the voice of shame is back, reminding us of our brokenness once again. In the end, it does us no good to argue with our shame.

Because it's not an argument we can win.

As the cold wind bites through my rock star costume, the voice of shame reminds me of unfamiliar grade school playgrounds and my all too familiar loneliness. And I'm tempted to argue back—to get lost in the same old never-ending cycle of debate with my shame. But instead, on this night, I close my inner mouth and open my inner ear. Instead of talking back to my shame, I listen for *another* voice—the voice of the spark—the voice I call grace. And on this night, I hear it, whispering at the center of me. Grace doesn't try to challenge the half-truth claims of my shame. Instead, the voice of grace reminds me of the whole truth: *You* do *look ridiculous, Kelly.* And *you are beautiful and beloved. You* aren't *the cool kid, Kelly—you never were.* And *you are beautiful and beloved. You* aren't *the most popular guy here tonight, Kelly.* And *you are beautiful and beloved.*

The voice of grace doesn't challenge the story I've been told by my shame—it totally subverts it by reminding me of the *rest* of the story. The voice of grace doesn't try to disprove the voice of shame. It doesn't do a *Yeah, but.* It does a *Yes, and.* It disrupts all the internal debates, undermines all the second-guessing, and avoids all the inner conflict. It says, *Yes, that may be true, and this is* definitely *true.* Grace tells you you're a mess and also lovely, broken and also beautiful, full of darkness and also light. Grace is the love that sees the ugly along with the beautiful, and joyfully holds both together in a tender embrace.

This is the voice of grace:

The kids on the playground think you're a nerd and no one wants to hang out with you . . . *and* you are beautiful and beloved. The girls at school are calling you chubby . . . *and* you are beautiful and beloved. The cuts on your arms advertise the torment you carry within . . . *and* you are beautiful and beloved. You keep losing weight but you still can't stand the sight of yourself in the mirror and you're scared of where this might end . . . *and* you are beautiful and beloved. You give yourself away to men and you can no longer look at your reflection in the mirror . . . *and* you are beautiful and beloved. You burned the dinner and the house is a mess and everyone is disappointed in you . . . *and* you are beautiful and beloved. You lost your job and you're struggling to provide for your family . . . *and* you are beautiful and beloved. No matter *what* . . . you are beautiful and beloved.

Someone once told me words are containers and what they contain is meaning. Over time, a word-container can get filled up with all sorts of different meanings, until the word itself becomes a jumble of muddled connotations, thus losing its meaning altogether. When this happens, if we want the word to have meaning again, we have to empty the word-container and refill it with clearer meaning.

Grace is a word-container overflowing with contradictory connotations.

And I had to empty it before I could fill it back up with love.

When I was young—back in the days of Sunday school flannel boards and youth groups and college and textbooks and infatuation with my intellect—grace was a container that got filled up with abstract concepts, theological doctrines, and intellectual ideas like transaction and debt and fairness. Grace was eternal forgiveness, of which no one was worthy. Grace was a heavenly escape hatch from the consequences of our foundational badness. Ironically, this word about God's love became a container for the language of unworthiness—it defined people as shameful and confined them to their brokenness. When I was a boy, grace was a word that made me want to hide myself from everyone—including myself—so it lost its power to transform me.

For years, I couldn't truly experience grace because I was so focused on trying to explain it. The voice of grace was whispering and waiting within me, but to encounter it, I had to stop looking for labels and start listening for love. I had to stop analyzing and start hearing. Then one blessed morning—on a Marine base in Virginia—I finally did: I quit asking about grace, and I started listening to it. I finally *experienced* grace and the word got emptied of its meaning and filled back up again, all at the same time. I'll tell you that story later in these pages, but right now what I'll tell you is this: when grace has shown you the light underneath your underneath, grace no longer feels like a love you don't deserve; it feels like a joyous embrace of what is truest about you.

I used to believe grace was a way of being saved; now I know grace is a way of being *seen*. Grace isn't an idea or a doctrine or an escape hatch. It's not a noun at all. Grace is a *verb*. Grace is a *happening*. Grace is what happens when that gentle voice inside us—and the tender voices around us—tell us about the beautiful soul we *already are*, regardless of how much mess we are covered with.

When I was a boy, grace was a word that harbored shame. Now, grace is a word-container overflowing with other words like acceptance, worthiness, and embrace. Grace used to be a word that made me want to hide from people; now it's a word that makes me want to *love* them.

I don't know what meaning your grace container has been filled with. Maybe it's filled with religious agendas or shaming theology or wounds inflicted by an institution aiming for holiness and so often missing the mark. If so, it need not remain that way. Empty it out. And then let it be filled back up with the voice that sees all your mess *and* all your beauty.

When we stop trying to explain grace and simply let it see us and speak to us, strange and beautiful things start to happen within us. A pressure at the back of the eyes. A subtle swelling in the chest. A small fluttering in the stomach. A little one inside of us, hopping from foot to foot, antsy with anticipation, preparing to run free.

Shame is a full-body experience, but grace is too.

All you have to do is allow it. Let hope take up residence in your heart. Let the tears come. Let the joy swell. Let your relief flutter and perhaps even take flight. Let the weight of a lifetime slide right off your shoulders. Until, finally, one night you let yourself sit in a ballroom looking ridiculous amongst your respectably clad peers, but feeling peaceful, even joyful, hearing only the voice of grace, and knowing you are good enough.

Because, no matter what, you are beautiful and beloved.

CHAPTER 12

Worthiness Isn't Being Cocky
(It's Being Honest)

What we are is God's gift to us.

ELEANOR POWELL

*E*very Friday morning for five years, I rose before the sun, gathered whatever book I was reading, along with a small black journal and a pen, and drove to a nearby coffee shop. I drank medium roast, ate oatmeal, read about the spiritual life, and recorded my own musings. On those quiet mornings, as my pen met the page, something stirred within me. It felt like joy.

It was the sensation of worthiness.

On those mornings, I wanted to race home and read what I'd written to my wife. A couple of times I did, and she lit up with joy too. But mostly, I just filled up my bedside table with unread pages, and I kept silent. Sharing my delight about what was inside of me felt boastful. Prideful. Perhaps even, in the language of my youth, a deadly sin.

In the first act of our story, for a while, shame renders us incapable of glimpsing our worthiness at all. But at some point—if we are listening for the voice of grace—we begin to see our worthiness more clearly, more frequently, and for longer periods of time. Then shame adopts another strategy: the impulse to cover our worthiness back up. At some point, shame ceases to be the feeling that we aren't enough, and becomes the urge to *bury* our enough-ness.

Inside the bedside table of our hearts.

As a therapist, I watch it happen almost every day. A good soul—just beginning to delight in itself—shares something about its beauty. Something about which it is proud, in the holiest and most innocent sense of the word. The soul speaks and the flesh that contains this lovely soul begins to mirror its joy—eyes get a little sparkle in them, the corners of lips curve ever so slightly upward, an entire being gets a little more animated. I watch the joy of worthiness overcoming all the conditioning that says we aren't supposed to delight in who we are.

But then the shame training kicks in.

Sheepishness quickly returns. Eyes are cast downward. Lips straighten out and clamp down. Muttered apologies are issued. The moment of joy gets minimized. Retracted. Qualifications are made. Self-negation replaces self-revelation. Worthiness is buried once again in the bedside table of a human heart, and I try to reach for the drawer before it snaps completely shut. I tell this good soul I was enjoying hearing about its worthiness—I was delighting in its beauty too—and I wonder why it so swiftly went back into hiding. Invariably, the answer comes back: it's arrogant to reveal the things about which you are proud—my parents said so, my peers think so, and my pastor taught me so. It's cocky to believe, let alone *say*, good things about yourself.

After five years of Friday mornings at the coffee shop, on a Friday in January 2012, everything changed. It started out like any other Friday morning. I woke up. I drank coffee and ate oatmeal. I wrote in my journal. And I went home. But then I pushed back against my lifelong instinct to hide myself away, and I gave in to the joy rustling within my soul. I decided to open up my bedside table and show my words to whoever was willing to read them.

I published my first blog post.

At first, it felt arrogant to boldly share my thoughts as if someone might actually be interested in hearing them. It felt cocky to talk about my experiences as if they might reveal something true. It felt prideful to act like there was something inside of me worth showing to the world. I worried about people criticizing the content of my words, but mostly I was afraid of people criticizing my audacity to *share* them.

Yet I let myself be guided by what I know about healing: at first, healing doesn't feel very healthy. When we've inverted right and wrong, good and bad, moral and immoral, then to do the healthy thing feels really wrong in the beginning. When you've been trained to be quiet, speaking up feels arrogant. When you've been trained to hide yourself, revealing yourself feels cocky. When you've been trained to bury who you are in a bedside table, opening up feels terribly self-centered.

The irony, though, is that by trying to protect ourselves against pride in this way, we are committing a different kind of transgression: we are lying. We're lying because, by burying our goodness inside of us, we are deceiving everyone. Including ourselves.

So one week after the first post, I published a second post. And then a week later, a third post. Each week, I sat down to write, wondering if I'd find more words to say. And every time, I did. Every time, the words arrived, like something happening to me and through me. By the fourth week, I was beginning to understand the strange paradox every writer eventually embraces: yes, I'm a good writer, but I'm also merely transcribing the word-gifts given to me every week.

This is, indeed, the strange paradox we all face if we choose to risk a little holy pride by taking our worthiness out of whatever bedside table we've been stashing it in: we are, each of us, something very, very good. And at the same time, the very good thing we are is also a gift. No more. No less. But absolutely *enough*.

The paradox that our goodness was given to us saves us from toxic pride.

When we take too much credit for the good thing we are, we develop the delusion we are self-made, in control of all things, and someone to be reckoned with. This is the toxic kind of pride, and usually when it speaks up, it puts others *down*. But once we know our goodness is a gift—once we know we are especially worthy but not particularly special—we begin to suspect everyone else has been gifted with goodness, as well. We want to speak up for ourselves, *and* we want to speak up for others.

Which is why the holy kind of pride never puts people down; it always lifts them up.

I'm glad Jesus had enough holy pride to speak up and lift up all of humanity out of its shame. I'm glad Abraham Lincoln had enough holy pride to speak up and lift up an entire race of people out of slavery. I'm glad Winston Churchill had enough holy pride to speak up and lift up a whole race of people out of genocide. I'm glad the Reverend Martin Luther King Jr. had enough holy pride to speak up and lift up an entire nation out of its institutionalized oppression.

I'm glad right now, on a playground somewhere, there is a kid who has enough holy pride to speak up and lift up another kid who doesn't know it's okay to speak up for himself. I'm glad my wife spoke up. I'm glad my therapist spoke up. I'm glad my spiritual mentors spoke up—I'm glad C. S. Lewis and Philip Yancey and Thomas Merton and Henri Nouwen and Richard Rohr and Gregory Boyle had enough holy pride to write about life and about love.

In your first act, as you hear the voice of grace with increasing clarity and consistency, there will eventually come a time—and perhaps for you it has already come—when you are ready to open the bedside table, take out the parts of you that you've hidden there, and begin showing them to the world. There will come a time when the little one inside of you is ready to trade in his or her well-learned false humility for the holy kind of pride, which knows you are good, but also knows that goodness is a gift. Then you will feel increasingly free to walk through this life bearing the gifts of your goodness and giving them away.

Because you know they are not yours to hold on to.

CHAPTER 13

You Are a Somebody
(and So Is Everybody Else)

*Perhaps together, we can teach each other how to
bear the beams of love, persons becoming persons,
right before our eyes. Returned to ourselves.*

GREGORY BOYLE

The day the film crew arrived at our house, I felt like a *somebody*.

It had been eight months since my daughter and I appeared on the *TODAY* show, and a film crew was flying to Chicago to interview me for a documentary about fathers and daughters and body image. Eight months earlier, facing the bright lights of Rockefeller Center, I'd awoken feeling insignificant and unimportant. On this morning, though, I awoke feeling like I was a big deal. The crew was scheduled to arrive within the hour, but I still needed to drop off three kids at two different schools and pick up breakfast for the crew. I was in a hurry and I was, obviously, the most important person on the road.

Unfortunately, the other motorists hadn't gotten the memo.

They didn't part like the Red Sea for me. They just puttered around, going to and from their ordinary destinations, blocking me from my extraordinary one. I cursed under my breath as I swerved around someone who clearly wasn't scheduled to be in a movie. A whimper from the back seat made me look in the rearview mirror. My kids' wide-eyed expressions said, *Uh-oh, Dad has lost it again. I don't know why, but Dad has definitely lost it again.*

I needed to calm down.

I tried to remind myself the people on the road were not roadblocks but people—people who also had important places to go. Yet on this morning, the voice of comparison in my head could not be silenced. It retorted, *Yeah, sure, but not as important as a filming!* The voice of comparison in me believes worthiness is relative. It tells me importance is a finite resource—if I'm important then someone else must be less important, and vice versa. It is, really, just the cleverly disguised voice of shame. And it's an awfully difficult voice to ignore, even after you've heard the voice of grace whispering of your worthiness.

I hit the accelerator, veered violently onto a side street, and tried not to notice my kids' eyes growing even larger.

Social psychologists say we compare ourselves to others for all sorts of reasons—self-understanding, self-verification, self-enhancement—but they all boil down to this: we're trying to figure out how much we're worth. Kids compare themselves based on how quickly they get picked in gym class and who gets to sit at the cool kids' table. Siblings compare who gets the most presents and the most love. By high school, adolescents spend more time comparing than studying.

Then we grow up, and we become spouses who fight over who's contributing most and who's loving best. Men compare themselves to each other, trying to figure out who is the better breadwinner.

And when a woman walks in the room, every other woman looks her up and down. But they're not judging her; they're judging themselves *relative* to her. We are constantly evaluating others in an effort to clarify our own self-worth. Is it any wonder our fragile sense of worth fluctuates like the stock market?

Is it any wonder we see, everywhere, roadblocks instead of people?

As I veered onto the side street, hoping I wouldn't have to deal with the rest of humanity for a few blocks, I saw it. Halfway down the block—with no possible detours between it and me—was a short yellow school bus parked on the side of the road. As I hit the accelerator and closed the distance, its red stop sign slowly—oh so achingly slowly—swung outward. I came to a halt, cursing under my breath. Which is when I saw them.

A young mother, tenderly helping her disabled daughter onto the bus.

I watched the young girl struggle to climb the stairs. Meanwhile, the red flashing stop sign blinked back at me. *Stop. Stop. Stop.* I watched the bus driver get up from his seat to help her. *Stop. Stop. Stop.* Somewhere inside me, something started to shift. I watched him slowly—oh so achingly slowly—walk with her to the rear of the bus. *Stop. Stop. Stop.* Somewhere inside me, something dislodged and fell. I watched him help her into her seat, fasten her seat belt, check twice to be sure she was safe. *Stop. Stop. Stop.* Somewhere inside me, something landed and split open. I watched him amble back to his driver's seat, the red light still flashing at me: *Stop. Stop. Stop.*

I watched the stop sign fold back into place on the side of the bus. The driver lifted his hand to wave me by. I shook my head. Kept my foot on the brake. Waved him ahead. I'd gotten the message: *Stop. Stop. Stop.*

Stop comparing, Kelly. And start seeing.

Social psychologists say our minds are wired for comparison, and they're right—our minds *are* wired to compare. The mind divides. It speaks the language of either-or. The mind turns worthiness into a lifelong contest and makes everybody an opponent, and we can't change the nature of our minds. But we *can* turn from our either-or thinking and listen to something else instead. Every time we hear the voice of comparison within us, we can listen once again for the voice of grace.

Our inciting incident begins the moment we first recognize, allow, and receive the gift of grace. But it doesn't end there. As the voice of grace assures us of our worthiness, we continue to listen, and grace begins to tell us something more. Something even better. Grace tells us we are unconditionally worthy, and the same is true of everyone else as well. Having been seen well by grace, we are freed to see well *with* grace. Our inner voice becomes our inner *eye*.

Something happened on that quiet side street.

A tectonic shift happened inside of me, and it didn't change my mind; it returned me to my soul. I didn't start thinking differently; I started *seeing* differently. I started seeing clearly. The voice of grace within me reminded me of what is true of all of us: we're broken *and* we're beautiful.

I saw a little girl hobble from her home, and I saw myself in her.

I saw that hobbling is holy.

I saw a tiny yellow school bus, and I saw myself in it.

I saw that smallness is sacred.

Eight months before the little yellow bus, as we arrived on the set of the *TODAY* show, I was mostly at peace with what was about to happen. Yet, every few minutes, a wave of anxiety would hit the shore of my heart, causing it to skip a beat.

When I saw the couch, though, the anxiety went away for good.

As a cameraman walked my daughter and me onto the set and toward the famous orange couch where we would be interviewed by Willie Geist and Natalie Morales, I was expecting luxury. But the couch was not luxurious. In fact, it was a little threadbare and tattered, even discolored in places. It was far from perfect and glamorous. It was just a normal couch and it gave me permission, finally, to be just a normal dad.

I think we're all like that couch, actually. When the bright lights are up and the camera is rolling, we put on our best face and look like we've got it all together, but when you look a little more closely, we're all a little worn and broken and tattered. We try to deny that reality, afraid of being frayed, thinking our stains make us less worthy. But the truth is, our fallibility is the common ground upon which all of us can actually take a seat, relax, look at each other, and say, "I'm a mess, but I'm still worthy. And so are you."

I have another couch that reminds me of that every day.

The couch in my therapy office has heard thousands of stories. It has heard the stories of powerful executives and powerless immigrants, stories of wild success and woeful failure, stories of the wealthy and the impoverished, stories of sorrow and joy, stories of rage and peace. It has heard threats of suicide and the grief of the terminally ill. It has heard every kind of story and, if it could speak, it would tell you the one thing every story has in common: every story is a *broken* story. And they are broken stories not because they're *therapy* stories but because they are *human* stories.

When you look closely, we're all a little broken.

Peter Rollins tells the parable of a rich Texas oilman who discovers he has a long-lost cousin in Ireland named Seamus, whom he then travels to meet. When the oilman arrives, Seamus begins showing his rich cousin around his humble property. After the short tour, the oilman boasts, "You should see my land in Texas. I can't even drive my car to the edges of it." Seamus hears his comparison and recognizes it for what it is—competition, bluster, and self-promotion. And he sees the fractured humanity it is meant to obscure. So, Seamus looks at his cousin, nods in understanding, and says, "Yeah, my car is broken too."

As our inciting incident unfolds and grace becomes the eye with which we see the world, as well as ourselves, comparison gives way to communion. Our minds give way to our hearts. The mind is complicated, but the heart is not. When our minds crack, they fall apart, but when our hearts break, they break open. And when our hearts break open, they get flooded by *commonality*.

When we allow our inner voice to become our inner eye, we begin to trust-fall from a psychology of competition into a spirituality of commonality. It is a spirituality of fallibility, of broken ground, which is always common ground and, thus, holy ground. Our mutual fallibility and fragility become the bread and wine of our communion. We trust-fall into our common ground and, when we land, we discover we've fallen right into the arms of our worthiness, and the worthiness of everyone around us.

We're all broken cars.

We're all tattered couches.

We're all disabled little ones on the way to the school bus.

"The human eye was never designed to look up in a way that

inflates the Other to superiority, nor to look down, reducing the Other to inferiority," writes poet John O'Donohue. "To look someone in the eye is a nice testament to truth, courage, and expectation. Each one stands on common, but different, ground."

You can quit comparing.

They aren't you.

Only you are you.

Embrace who you are.

Then get ready to embrace everyone else.

Your second act is waiting for you.

A Father's Letter to His Daughter
(about the Worthiness of Everyone)

Dear Little One,

At 5:00 a.m. on the morning you and I went on the *TODAY* show, while you were still sleeping in the hotel room with Momma and your brothers, I left the hotel and set out on foot into the dark streets of Manhattan. I was looking for a cheap breakfast. But I was looking for something else as well.

I was looking for peace.

Sweetie, I was scared, because when I woke up I had looked in the mirror and staring back at me was a regular dad, an unremarkable psychologist, and a blogger who'd written the right letter to you at the right time. We were about to go on national television, share a stage with famous actors, and answer the questions of famous newscasters. How could I compare?

I found a Starbucks and, inside of it, I found our breakfast.

And my answer.

I placed my order for smoothies with the bleary-eyed barista, and in the stillness of the empty café, my anxiety screeched within me. Instead of fighting it, I allowed it, and I tried to listen for my trusted companion—the voice within me I call grace. I was waiting for the voice of grace to remind me that I'm good enough. But on this morning, it didn't speak to me about *my* worthiness; it spoke to me about the *barista's* worthiness: *This four minutes is just as important as your four minutes on television. And this young man is just as important as all those famous people you'll meet today.*

The voice of grace does that sometimes. It reminds me I don't need to do anything or earn anything or prove anything or look a certain way or say a certain thing in order to be worthy. And then it reminds me if this is true of me, then it is true of everyone else as well. It reminds me we're all just people trying to figure out what it means to be human. It shows me we're all living and breathing on the same level playing field, no matter how many hierarchies we imagine.

How could I compare to all those famous people? I couldn't. The truth is, none of us can be compared to anyone else. We are, each one of us, unique and lovely beings. Life isn't about comparison; it's about connection. Some of us forget this. I certainly do. But in the dark hours of a Thursday morning in Manhattan, I was reminded once again. And when you're reminded, all you want to do with your one unique and lovely life is help other people remember too.

So I asked the barista his name, and I asked him about his morning. We talked for a while, two human beings doing our best to be human together. No competition. No comparison. Only connection. And as we connected, I knew the people I'd be seeing later in the day were just as worthy as this young man. And just as worthy as me. Not more. Not less. The same.

My anxiety stopped screeching.

Sweetie, I fell in love with you when you were still just a cluster of cells inside your momma's tummy. Before you had a body, I loved the way you looked. Before you had a mind, I loved the way it thought. Before you had a heart, I embraced the speed of its tenacious beat. You are forever beautiful, Little One. *And so is everyone else.* If you listen to the voice inside of you that reminds you of this truth, your life will become a gift to the world. And you will have peace. The kind of peace that can withstand the lowlights.

And the bright lights.

Peace to you,

Daddy

—— *Act Two:* *Belonging* ——

You Are Not Alone

To be yourself in a world that is constantly
trying to make you something else is
the greatest accomplishment.

RALPH WALDO EMERSON

A Daddy's Letter to His Little Girl
(about Her Future Husband)

Dear Cutie-Pie,

Recently, your mother and I were searching for an answer on Google. Halfway through entering the question, Google returned a list of the most popular searches in the world. Perched at the top of the list was "How to keep him interested."

It startled me. I scanned several of the countless articles about how to be sexy and sexual, when to bring him a drink versus a sandwich, and the ways to make him feel smart and superior.

And I got *angry.*

Little One, it *is* not, never *has been,* and never *will be* your job to "keep him interested."

Little One, your only task is to know deeply in your soul—in that unshakeable place that isn't rattled by rejection and loss and ego—that you are worthy of interest. (If you can remember that everyone else is worthy of interest also, the battle of your life will be mostly won.) Remember, relationships aren't about *proving* your worth; they are about *revealing* your worth and, thus, finding the people who *see* your worth.

If you can trust your worth in this way, you will be attractive in the most important sense of the word: you will attract a boy who is both *capable* of interest and who wants to spend his one life investing his interest in *you.*

Little One, I want to tell you about the boy who doesn't need to be kept interested, because he knows you are interesting:

I don't care if he puts his elbows on the dinner table—as long as he puts his eyes on the way your nose scrunches when you smile. And then can't stop looking.

I don't care if he can't play a bit of golf with me—as long as he can play with the children you give him and revel in all the glorious and frustrating ways they are just like you.

I don't care if he doesn't follow his wallet—as long as he follows his *heart* and it always leads him back to you.

I don't care if he is strong—as long as he gives you the space to exercise the strength that is in *your* heart.

I couldn't care less how he votes—as long as he wakes up every morning and daily elects you to a place of honor in your home and a place of reverence in *his* heart.

I don't care about the color of his skin—as long as he paints the canvas of your lives with brushstrokes of patience, and sacrifice, and vulnerability, and tenderness.

I don't care where he was raised, as long as he was raised to value the sacred and to know every moment of life, and every moment of life with you, is *deeply* sacred.

In the end, Little One, if you stumble across a boy like that and he and I have nothing else in common, we will have the most important thing in common: *you.*

Because in the end, Little One, the only thing you should have to do to "keep him interested" is to be you.

Your eternally interested guy,

Daddy

— CHAPTER 14 —

Why Loneliness Happens, How We Make It Worse, and What We Can Do to Make It Better

All I ever wanted was to belong,
to wear that hat of belonging.

ANNE LAMOTT

Loneliness happens.

It is as much a part of life as hunger and sunsets and funerals. It is simply what happens when we grow up and realize we have a universe inside of us to which no other person has access, and that every other person contains an unknowable universe as well. Loneliness is an unavoidable thing and—though it is usually unpleasant and sometimes quite painful—it might even be an essential thing, because it can become the seed of *holy* things, like our craving for connection, our urge to belong, and our impulse to reach out and to reach *up*. Loneliness is the seed from which true togetherness can spring, if we cease to hide it and learn to reveal it, if we cease to be ashamed of it and learn to be connected in the midst of it. Instead of seeking to be rescued *from* our loneliness, we can seek to be joined *in* it.

113

This, of course, is far easier said than done.

Because most of us, as a little one, experienced a moment (or moments) in which we revealed who we truly were, made ourselves known, put ourselves out there, sought connection, and were left lonely anyway. Reflexively and unconsciously, we concluded our true self was the cause of our loneliness. We decided our true self was not worthy of closeness and togetherness, not worthy of belonging. So we began building *another* self. A false self. Then we buried our true self beneath it.

Though we have no idea we've done it.

Aidan didn't know he couldn't see well until after he *could*.

As a toddler, he was a little clumsy. He bumped into stuff, tripped a lot, and couldn't catch a ball very well. I was an athlete as a kid, but it seemed he wasn't going to be one. I loved him anyway and thought no more of it.

Until a routine vision screening in preschool.

The screening revealed a condition called amblyopia, or lazy eye. It turns out not all lazy eyes look lazy; some just *act* lazy. When he was born, his brain began to rely more on his left eye than his right. As a result, the vision in his right eye gradually deteriorated. By the time he was tested, he was almost blind in that eye.

Why didn't Aidan tell us he was going blind?

Because he couldn't remember what it was like to see clearly. To him, blurriness was business as usual. He was blind to the fact that he was blind. He simply couldn't see what he couldn't see.

Our true self and our false self work the same way.

We gradually quit using our true self, like a weak right eye, while we begin to build and strengthen another self—our false self.

The little one in us shrinks back into the shadows, and a bigger, less vulnerable kid takes over. The false self is the guardian of the true self. It's the safe self. Our protector. Its job is to help us find the belonging we believe our true self would never be able to achieve on its own. As our minds increasingly rely on the false self, it grows stronger and we grow increasingly dependent upon it.

We all have amblyopia of the self.

We stumble through life, seeing only through our false self, bumping into people, hurting ourselves, dropping the ball in our relationships, and adding a loneliness of our own making to the normal, inevitable loneliness of being alive. Yet we have no idea we're doing it. We cannot remember what it was like to see with our true self, so our false self seems like business as usual.

We simply don't know what we aren't seeing about who we are.

When Aidan put eyeglasses on, he finally saw the world clearly. But he saw something else too: he saw how *little* he had been seeing of the world all along. Our inciting incident is like putting on glasses for the first time—we hear the voice of grace and it shows us the true self we've become blind to. It awakens us to who we truly are. But in doing so, it also awakens us to who we are not. Because the moment we catch a glimpse of our true self, we can finally see our false self for what it is. A persona. A facade.

It can be a little disorienting.

The second act of our story usually begins with a bit of emotional vertigo as it dawns on us that what we thought was true is really false and what we couldn't remember existed is the truest thing of all. My second act vertigo began with a Marine base and a blank greeting card . . .

For the first three decades of my life, I unknowingly put my false self in charge of making me unlonely. I figured out how to read people and give them what they wanted, because usually when someone is pleased *by* you they are also pleased *with* you. It didn't work. My loneliness grew. So, instead, I puffed myself up, reciting political ideology and religious theology, trying to command belonging by appearing right and righteous. That didn't work either. So then I got married, hoping it would fix my loneliness problem. But it didn't. It *couldn't.* Because by the time I got married, my true self was so deeply buried, nothing and no one could connect with it. Yet I was oblivious to the entire drama.

Because sometimes you don't know what you're not seeing.

Between the mental effort required to predict what everyone wanted of me, the intensity of my ideological devotions, and the energy it took to contain my disappointment in people, I was utterly exhausted. And utterly lonely. Because the sad irony is, our false self dooms us to the fate it was created to avoid.

Thank God for Marine Corps Base Quantico.

We were there for my sister-in-law's wedding, and it was a joyful celebration. Yet as family and friends danced together well into the night, my loneliness only deepened. So as I fell asleep, I bitterly resorted to my default: I blamed my wife for not attending to me closely enough.

The next morning was Father's Day, and I awoke in the dark hours, steeped in disappointment and resentment. Yet this particular morning arrived at the end of a long and slow accumulation of experiences—a first act lasting many, many months, in which I'd begun to cultivate the capacity for stillness and for listening to my inner voices. Mostly I'd been hearing my shame, but there had been other moments too—moments in which I'd sensed a murmur of something else. Who can comprehend the mystery of the moment a life changes? Did I choose that particular morning, or did the morning choose me? Maybe it's as simple as this: we finally suffer enough to give up and give in to the inciting incident we didn't even know was possible.

I got out of bed and went down to the hotel lobby.

Instead of blaming, I listened.

My inciting incident happened as I heard clearly, for the very first time, the voice of grace whispering within me, a gentle whisper that put eyeglasses on my soul. I saw my true self. Grace showed me the light underneath my underneath. I saw my anger with new eyes, and I experienced it as a breadcrumb back toward my true self. I experienced my belovedness as a fact rather than a transient state of being hinging on every win and loss. I saw a soul with infinite value sitting at the center of me, and I knew its value could not be increased or decreased, no matter how much stuff I bought. I saw, mirrored back to me, a beauty that doesn't age, wrinkle, or die. I saw the little one I had been, timid and scared, but whole and ready to grow up and grow into his true self. My craving for the worthiness-whisper of my wife subsided, satisfied by the worthiness-whisper happening within me. I knew I was a wreck *and* I was worthy, and as the day dawned and the lobby began to fill with people, I knew without a doubt that each of them was just as worthy as me.

It was a liberation—like I was walking, finally, out of a jail cell in which I'd been imprisoned. Yet, ironically, I still couldn't see what had been imprisoning me. I returned to my family—a great light pulsing at the center of me—and joyfully packed the car for the final leg of our road trip. Before I started the car, my wife handed me a Father's Day present: two Bob Dylan albums. For my wife, listening to Bob Dylan is torture—sonic waterboarding—so two new Dylan albums at the beginning of a long car trip was a pure, intentional sacrifice. A true gift.

But there was a problem.

In the rush to pack the family and get us halfway across the country, she had forgotten to sign the card. No thoughtful words. No assurance of my worthiness. No guarantee of my belonging. Suddenly, the new joy with which I had returned to my family was competing with an old resentment. After my inciting incident, *I* knew I was worthy, but did *my wife* know it? It seemed she didn't.

My defensive and angry false self rose up within me. Yet for the first time, it wasn't the only thing I could see. For the first time in my life, standing on the solid ground of my true self, I could see my false self for what it was: not me, but a *creation* of mine. The curtain had been pulled back on the Wizard of Oz. I could finally see the real, ordinary man behind the curtain—and I kind of liked him! Which meant I could now also see the smoke and mirrors and violence of my false self as exactly that: false. At last I could see what I had not been seeing.

And I had a choice to make.

I could step back into the prison cell of my false self—resenting and blaming my wife for not making me feel worthy—or I could listen to the voice of grace and trust that my worthiness was absolute. It was nobody's responsibility to increase it for me, and nobody could decrease it for me either. I could choose to let my false self go to battle for me, or I could invite the little one inside of me to come out and play.

On that particular morning, I chose to play.

I listened to Dylan and I was grateful for my wife's gift and, suddenly, in our marriage, a space was opened that had previously been filled by my resentment. As the miles rolled by, my wife and I filled up that space with laughter and love instead. And as we put the miles behind us, I put a little more of my loneliness behind me too. Not all of it. Never all of it. But for a day, it stopped driving me.

For a day, my loneliness took a back seat to my belonging.

Director and screenwriter Steven Spielberg once said, "People have forgotten how to tell a story. Stories don't have a middle or an end anymore. They usually have a beginning that never stops beginning." In the story of our lives, it's tempting to do the same thing—to tell a story with an endless beginning. Now that we can hear the voice of grace and have a steady, sneaking suspicion we might actually be worthy, a part of us will want to remain there, to simply enjoy our enough-ness, and set up camp in act one. It's safe. Secure. There is no risk.

Except there is.

It's the risk of not finding the people to whom you belong.

You're wired to belong, to enter into community, to join and be joined, to be one with something bigger than yourself. You're wired for relationship. The second act of life is when you find your people and begin to truly enjoy them. But like the good second act of any story, it won't be easy—you face danger, the action rises, the stakes get higher, the subplots get complicated, and the tension ratchets up.

In act two, you find true belonging by learning how to hold on to your worthiness while venturing out into a world that seems to be doing its best to take it from you. You increasingly tune your ears to the frequency of grace, which is steadily broadcasting your worthiness through the unrelenting static of shame. You let the voice of grace teach you about your false self and how to let it go, over and over again, so you might actually live and love from your true self. It's a chance to set real boundaries for a change, rather than putting up walls that hide who you are. It's a chance to stand up to the bullies, to walk away from the sticks and the stones, to step out and show up, to apologize, to forgive, to release the people who continue to wound you, to ask for help, and ultimately to find your people by announcing who you are.

It's a chance to transform your loneliness into togetherness.

In the second act of life, you walk into the sturdy shed of the false self and roll out your true self, like an old dusty bike that hasn't been ridden in years. You start to pedal, teeter for a little while, and then gather speed, remembering what it feels like to ride with the wind on your face. On a downhill slope.

On a day when the sunlight is, finally, brighter than your shame.

CHAPTER 15

A Castle, a Chrysalis, a Tomb, and a Bodyguard

Friendship with one's self is all important,
because without it one cannot be friends
with anyone else in the world.

ELEANOR ROOSEVELT

I'm actually not wild about the term "false self."

It sounds like something you might wipe off like makeup, or take off like a Halloween mask. But the false self is a magnificent, complex, and resilient creation. We are much more likely to become lost in it and imprisoned by it than to shed it like extra clothing. The phrase simply doesn't do justice to the magnitude of our other self. Which is why I tend to use a different word for the false self. I call it what it is.

Ego.

I first came face-to-face with my ego on a Marine base.

So, naturally, I decided to declare war on it.

In the ensuing months and years, I watched my ego rise up

within me over and over again. When my wife seemed to care more for her job than for me. When the kids didn't act like Father knows best. When a friend was slow to respond to a text. When I didn't feel like the best therapist in the world. It seemed someone was always letting me down or I was continually messing up, and my ego was on constant standby, ready to step in and protect the little one in me.

Again and again, as I watched my ego rise up in me, I also watched what it gave rise *to* in my life: in my fear I hid myself *away* from everyone else, in my judgment I set myself *apart* from everyone else, and in my arrogance I imagined myself well *above* everyone else. Away. Apart. Above. It was, ironically, a recipe for spectacular loneliness. So, as I watched my ego do its thing, I wanted to destroy it. Unfortunately, you can't declare war on the ego. Because war is what it's built for.

Whoops.

The ego isn't the psychological equivalent of an internal organ like a heart or a brain or a pancreas. You can't cut it out like a gallbladder. And because it isn't made of flesh and blood, it can feel like a bit of an enigma. Ephemeral, like a ghost. But the ego is exactly the opposite of a wispy specter. It's more like an impenetrable fortress.

The ego is like a castle with three parts: walls, cannons, and thrones.

Walls. When our tender hearts first experience rejection and shame, we build walls around our souls to keep people out and to keep ourselves safe—walls that look like silence and avoidance, or pretending and people-pleasing and public personas, or giving in and fitting in instead of standing up and standing out. Typically, our ego walls develop sometime in elementary school, right around the time we become aware other people can judge us and critique us and belittle us with a single word, or even a simple look.

Cannons. The walls of our ego are a good defense, but the best defense is a good offense, so we eventually add ego cannons to our ego walls. For some of us, ego cannons are violent—lots of fists and fury. But for most of us, ego cannons take on more socially acceptable guises: blame, condemnation, resentment, retaliation, and gossip, to name a few. My wife says men put cannons on their ego walls, but women are more likely to use archers—precision strikes that cut close to the bone. Our ego cannons (or arrows) usually develop sometime in late childhood or early adolescence.

Thrones. When our ego cannons inevitably backfire, leaving us lonelier than ever, we try a different tactic. We build ego thrones on which to sit, and we fancy ourselves royalty. We construct our thrones out of power, possessions, and prestige. We find something to win or someone to dominate. This typically happens in early adulthood, though sometimes sooner, sometimes later, and sometimes never.

All of this is completely normal—which is to say, completely human.

And it is also among the most common causes of suffering in the world. The self-protective ego keeps us isolated and alone, deprived of the authentic belonging we all desperately want and need. It creates division and leads to violence of one kind or another. It is the fuel of arrogance. It ruins marriages and families and relationships of every kind. It keeps us from knowing who we are, who our people are, and what we're here to do.

So I wanted to tear down my ego wall brick by brick, blow up my cannons, and take a sledgehammer to my throne. I wanted it all gone without a trace. But every time I used a full frontal attack to dismantle my ego—for instance, every time I beat myself up for blowing up, or knocked myself down for acting like I was above everyone else—I only strengthened my ego further. Because, ironically, I was trying to dismantle my ego with my ego. I had simply turned my cannons on myself, which meant my ego had found a way to feed on itself. Egos are sneaky that way. However, I did eventually find a way to deal with it. It turns out, we don't find freedom from our ego by hating it or attacking it; we find freedom by loving it and befriending it.

I befriended my ego around the time my son brought home a book called *Wonder*.

Wonder is the story of a ten-year-old boy named Auggie, born with extreme facial deformities. It's the tale of a boy beginning public school for the first time. Middle school is treacherous enough when you look completely normal. But for a kid with a misshapen head and facial features like running wax, middle school is like venturing into the wild, where your tender heart is the prey, and your peers are the predators. My son read the book first. The rumor going around his school was you couldn't read it without crying. He vowed not to crack, but he emerged from his bedroom with cheeks glistening. The same thing happened to my wife.

And it left me with glistening cheeks too.

As I read *Wonder*, I wanted desperately for Auggie to protect himself, to shield his lovely heart from the abuse of others, and, to my surprise, I was glad when his budding ego emerged. He would have been emotionally eviscerated without it. It was essential to the survival of his heart. It was a necessary armor, there to protect and preserve him, for a time, as he ventured through the wild.

After I read *Wonder*, I stopped hating my ego and became

grateful for it. Instead of declaring war on it, I started embracing it. And then, instead of trying to destroy it, I started saying *goodbye* to it, like a slow parting with an old friend you can always return to in your time of need. I learned you don't resist your ego; you release it. You don't tear down your castle; you walk out of it. In other words, while reading *Wonder*, I became aware of a part of the ego-castle I'd been overlooking: the drawbridge.

In a castle, the drawbridge is a point of vulnerability, a passageway through which the castle inhabitants have contact with the outside world, and one that permits the outside world to enter the castle. However, a drawbridge is always controlled from the inside. No one can force us to lower our defenses and step out of our ego. It's up to us to let down our drawbridge so our soul can roam freely.

Therapists rely a great deal on metaphors. Metaphors make it easier to name and understand the complicated and abstract realities of our inner universe. So we therapists tend to throw them around and mix them up at will. We'll draw on whatever images work. And while the castle metaphor can help us to *understand* the ego, it may not be the best metaphor to help us *befriend* the ego. After reading *Wonder*, I became fond of a few other metaphors for the ego: chrysalis, tomb, and bodyguard.

Chrysalis. Maybe our false self is not meant to be a fortress. Maybe it's meant to be like a thin membrane, protecting us during the process of becoming the beautiful creature we already are. It's a membrane that can't conceal our true self forever—it gives way once we experience the beauty we are beneath all the shame and protecting and pretending. When the urge to spread our wings and fly becomes absolutely insuppressible, the membrane bursts and then falls away.

Tomb. Or maybe the ego is like a tomb. We bury our true self inside of it, and our true self seems to be dead and gone forever. But then three days later—or three years or three decades or three whatevers later—we discover the stone has been rolled away, and our true self has gotten up and is walking around and is more radiant than ever. Maybe, like a tomb, the ego harbors our soul, preserving the soul for its resurrection, here, now, in *this* life.

Loyal bodyguard. Or perhaps the ego is like a loyal bodyguard—the muscle we hire to protect us when the world gets dangerous. And maybe rather than beating up on our bodyguard for doing the job we trained him or her to do, we need to thank our protector for a job well done.

These days, I call my ego Bruno.

I forgive Bruno for all the liberties he's taken when I wasn't looking. I apologize for the orders I've given him when I *was* looking. And I tell Bruno he can stand down now. And you know what? He almost always does. The problem is, he was made for protection, so when I stop keeping an eye on him, he goes back to work again.

There is, I think, some truth in each of these metaphors. Yet, there is one more metaphor which illustrates the process of releasing the ego with even more clarity. I discovered this metaphor a few summers ago. On a carnival ride with an anxious kid.

Who was clinging to a metal lap bar . . .

CHAPTER 16

How to Let Go of Your False Self

Some of us think holding on makes us strong; but sometimes it is letting go.

HERMANN HESSE

We have a rite of passage in our family.

It happens in Rehoboth Beach, Delaware, at a boardwalk carnival, on a ride called the Paratrooper. The Paratrooper is like a Ferris wheel on steroids. It whips you in a circle, diagonal to the ground, while your legs dangle beneath you. As it reaches its apex, you feel like you'll just keep going upward and be hurled into the ocean. The Paratrooper has a crossbar that runs across your lap. And *it* is the rite of passage.

We ride so we can let it go.

Though your every instinct is to endure the ride white-knuckled, with sweaty palms gripping the crossbar, the goal is to let go of the bar, raise your hands above your head, let loose a wild scream, and trust you'll be okay even when you feel like you'll be flung like a rag doll into the great blue yonder. The goal is to abandon yourself to the deepest thrill of the ride.

Three years ago, Quinn, who was five at the time, decided he was ready to try.

As the ride slowly commenced, he began to whimper. One circuit in and he was clinging desperately to the crossbar, his face as pale as his white knuckles. Two circuits in and he was gripping the bar so tightly I wondered if he would bend it in half. Letting go can feel like the scariest thing in the world.

And our egos are like that crossbar.

If a wild carnival ride didn't have a crossbar to hold you in, no one would participate—it would be deemed unwise and unsafe. At first, the ego serves the same essential and protective function—it wouldn't be wise or safe to start riding through this life without it. During our backstory and our first act, the ego serves a critical purpose: when it seems like we might soon be flung out into our ocean of shame, our ego gives us something to hold on to, something for the little one in us to cling to when the world seems too big to handle.

Eventually, though, the time comes to let it go.

On the Paratrooper, as the ride began to whip us skyward again, I whispered words of reassurance to Quinn. I told him I was with him, and I wasn't going anywhere. Slowly, he calmed down and his whimpering subsided. Some pink returned to the little knuckles on the crossbar next to me.

In the second act of life, the voice of grace continues to whisper of our worthiness, but now it begins whispering of something else as well. Like a loving parent, the voice of grace sits next to the scared little one inside of us and whispers, *I know you're afraid, but I'm right here. You're going to be all right. You don't need your ego anymore.*

You can let go now. In other words, in the second act of life, we are whispered into a rite of passage.

As we reached the top of the ride and the blue Atlantic Ocean sprawled out below us and the vast blue sky stretched out above us, Quinn's hands slowly rose off the crossbar. He was terrified as he reached for the endless sky, and he let loose a maniacal scream—half fear, half laughter, half relief.

Letting go of our ego feels a little crazy at first.

We could wait for our fear to go away before letting go. We could wait for some guarantee that people will see our worthiness and we will find a place to belong. But it simply doesn't work that way. Letting go doesn't come with a warranty. And it almost always happens timidly at first.

A tentative, shaky, halfhearted release.

As we descended again on the Paratrooper, Quinn's hands reflexively came down, and he reached for the crossbar again. This time, though, his hands rested there only a moment or two, and the white knuckles didn't return. Then, as the ride began another ascent, he released the bar again, stretching his hands high above his head. This time his laughter was mostly joy and delight.

The letting go of our false self happens like this, in fits and starts. Because when we let go of the ego, it doesn't go away; *we* go away from *it*. Like the crossbar, the false self is always there and we can always return to it when we choose to. But with each successive release, we begin to discover *we don't want to*. We begin to realize life is about embracing the risk and adventure and vulnerability of the ride we're on. It's about raising our hands over our heads and declaring, "Here I am, world!" We discover there is joy in letting go of our ego, because when we let it go, what remains is who we truly are.

And who we truly are is wild and good and free.

So if the crossbar is our ego, what does the ride itself represent?

It would be a little too easy to equate the ride with life. The much harder and more specific truth is, the ride is our relationships. The ride is *people*—lovers and lifelong companions, friends and foes, siblings and in-laws, the girl or the guy you're crushing on, your boss and your coworkers. It's the guy in the car next to you and the cashier at the supermarket. The ride is the constant, everyday confrontation with people who may or may not see you for the good thing you are.

But that's not the whole truth either.

The whole truth is, our relationships are just the context for the real confrontation. Really, the ultimate confrontation is not happening *between* people; it's happening *within* people. Having been protected by your ego for most of your life, the question central to the second act of your story is, will you confront your fear and your facade? Will you let go of the old safety mechanisms you've begun to outgrow? And will you choose new ways of caring for your soul in a world that is often unkind and sometimes even cruel? Will you learn more sincere ways of holding on to who you truly are, more loving ways of sheltering your heart from shame, and more vulnerable ways to be in relationship?

In the midst of this inner confrontation, we have an opportunity to learn an essential lesson about what it means to be human: the soul doesn't need an ego to do its dirty work—your true self can take care of itself, while still loving everyone else. Will you trust the voice of grace as it calls you into this second act of your story? Will you enter into your rite of passage? Because if you are willing to let go—if you are willing to raise your arms high and spread them wide—something beautiful awaits you. Something you are here to enjoy.

It is called belonging.

What If a Stiff Arm Is the Most Loving Thing You Can Give?

*Daring to set boundaries is about having
the courage to love ourselves, even when
we risk disappointing others.*

BRENÉ BROWN

The day my daughter first rejected me was one of the happiest days of my life.

The sun was just up, and I was returning home from the gym, expecting to find a still slumbering household. In the kitchen, dust motes were dancing silently in the early morning sunlight. Sitting there quietly, reading a book at the breakfast table, was five-year-old Caitlin. She'd woken earlier than usual, but I assumed the rest of our morning routine would be the same. So I went to her, planning to wrap her in a big hug. But when I got within arm's length, the ritual changed.

She stiff-armed me.

She put five years' worth of little-girl arm between us. And if it's possible, she stiff-armed me with her eyes too, while saying firmly, "No, thank you."

It took me by surprise and I stopped short. The dad in me was a little hurt—though it probably wasn't the *dad* in me; it was probably the *ego* in me. I get the two confused sometimes. The dad-ego in me wanted to push right past her boundary and wrap her in a big hug anyway. I could picture it. It would be funny and playful, and I suspected it would still end in laughter and smiles. Yet I didn't do it.

Because the *psychologist* in me wasn't hurt at all; he was thrilled!

The psychologist in me was ecstatic to see his daughter saying no, because he knows the inability to set personal boundaries is one of the most common, insidious causes of human suffering. He didn't always know it, though.

He didn't know it until he started asking a question.

As a psychologist, I've been exposed to all sorts of theories about the problems of being human. Sigmund Freud's theories intrigued me, so for a while I assumed everyone was struggling with deep, repressed sexual and aggressive impulses. And of course we are, but they aren't nearly as dramatic as Freud made them out to be. Then I learned about biology and temperament, and I figured everyone was just struggling to do the best they could with the cards they'd been dealt. I learned about behavioral theory, and I tried to help people cope more effectively with stress using relaxation techniques. Cognitive theory said bad feelings always result from wrong thinking. I was skeptical of that one, but I implemented its interventions anyway, because when you're in the trenches, you'll try anything.

In the end, though, experience won out over theories.

Over the years, I began to notice a common thread running through the painful fabric of my clients' lives. The people I worked with weren't primarily angry or sexually repressed or badly wired or breathing the wrong way or thinking the wrong things. They all had something *else* in common.

They didn't know how to say no.

Almost every client was having difficulty setting authentic, healthy boundaries. The problem was so pervasive that I needed to understand it better. I started asking questions and one question in particular: "How did your parents respond to you when you said no?" And almost invariably the answer would come back: "Oh, you wouldn't dare say no to *my* parents."

Our families are where we first learn how to say no in a safe and supportive environment. If we don't learn to do so there, it is difficult to learn it anywhere else. If children can't say no to a parent—the person who is supposed to be most patient with their becoming—they likely won't say it to anyone. And there is no end to the ways we are diminished by our inability to set boundaries.

We give in to the pressure of a friend, so we drink and drive and we endanger lives. We cave in constantly to a persuasive lover, so we drown in a sea of their wishes. We get taken in by a sales pitch, so we bury ourselves in oppressive debt. We get abused by a boss, so we end up with long hours at work and a short fuse at home. We cater to our kids' every need, so we wind up resenting their demands and even their presence. We submit to unhealthy partners and they keep drinking or working or gambling or flirting, so we end up together but utterly alone. We let everyone else tell us what story to live, and we cease to be the author of our own life. When we silence the boundaries our soul wants to set, we silence everything—the love our soul wants to give and the dreams it wants to live.

Am I suggesting children should say no to everything? Absolutely not. I'm saying they are *practicing*, and it is the responsibility of a parent to coach them. When a "no" looks more like a punch than a stiff arm—violent and oppositional and a no-for-the-sake-of-saying-no—it's an ego cannon learning how to fire, and kids need to learn a more loving way of preserving who they are. Yet, often, a budding ego takes a more quiet and submissive guise, saying yes to everyone around it. It's the ego's way of manipulating others into sticking around. At those times, kids need to be *encouraged* to say no.

Even to a parent.

By the time my daughter is old enough to be offered the back seat of a car on a Friday night date, I want her to have had *a lot* of practice at saying no. The day will come when there is more at stake than an early morning hug and, when that day comes, I want her to know she still has a place to belong even when she doesn't give herself away. I want her to know she doesn't have to get into the back seat of somebody else's life.

Because she's in the driver's seat of her own life.

So in an early morning standoff with little Caitlin, I was a dad-ego with his arms flung wide open, but I was also a psychologist-soul with his *eyes* wide open to the importance of this moment. I looked at her stiff arm and her strong eyes and her confident words, and I knew they were the best kind of boundary. They were the soul wearing a five-year-old body and wearing it well, asserting itself gently but firmly. The dad-ego in me was still tempted to push past her for his hug.

But the psychologist-soul in me stepped back.

Instead of keeping his arms wide open, he held his fist way out, knuckles first. He looked her in the eye and said, "Good for you, sweetie. You don't ever have to let anyone hug you if you don't want to. You can always trust your heart, like you did just now. You can let it speak for you."

My daughter reached out, fist closed. She gently tapped her knuckles against mine. The dust motes danced around us and our fist bump was a kind of dance too—the dance of two souls letting themselves be seen, not hiding behind an automatic "yes" or a violent "no," respecting the dignity of the other.

The space between us was the kind of space in which two souls can truly belong.

The serious look in her eyes dissolved. Her head tilted slightly. She looked at me thoughtfully. And then her eyes shone with a light brighter than the rays on the kitchen table as she flung her arms open wide for our usual morning hug. My daughter had to say no before she could truly say yes.

We all do.

A stiff arm gives us the kind of space to decide what we want, what we value, and what we will or will not let happen. Only after we've created space with a stiff arm—the space for our true self to decide what is the most loving thing to do for everyone involved, including itself—does a "yes" become a true "yes."

Perhaps you have a little one in you who was never allowed to say no. Or maybe the little one in you was shown how to say no with a clenched fist but not with a stiff arm. If so, it's going to be a little scary to let your soul speak and set a boundary for you, because you run the risk of disappointing people, offending them, and perhaps even making them angry. That's okay. In the first act of life, you learned to embrace yourself, but in this second act you learn you don't *have* to be embraced by everyone else. Which, of course, is a whole new way of embracing yourself. And it ensures every embrace you give is real, authentic, and mutual.

That is how belonging begins.

With an arm that's stiff.

And only *then* with arms open wide.

— CHAPTER 18 —

Maybe Heaven Really Is in Our Midst

The art of pleasing is the art of deception.

LUC DE CLAPIERS

This time, it's Aidan sitting at the kitchen table, and he's drawing a picture. I peer over his shoulder. It's not his typical subject matter—he's drawing a character from a television show he hasn't watched in years, and the strokes don't reflect his usual zeal. I ask him why he's drawing it. He tells me it's homework for school. He and his classmates were assigned to draw one of their favorite fictional characters, but he chose to draw one of his teacher's favorite characters instead. He's been trying to earn her approval for most of his fifth-grade year, to no avail. It appears he's now trying to earn it by being someone he is not. He's eleven years old

The hiding starts early.

⁓

"Same!"

It's a common refrain heard among adolescents. It's a teenager's way of saying, "Hey, I have the same interest or belief or blue jeans or favorite musician, so I must belong to you!" And if the match isn't perfect, well, they'll fudge a little bit, like suddenly falling in love with sports because the person they've fallen in love with is an athlete. Same! It's a shortcut to finding a place to belong. My son is beginning to use the shortcut. I have it memorized.

In college I majored in psychology, but in *life* I majored in people pleasing.

My parents liked it when I was funny, so I told lots of jokes. Same! My teachers liked it when I knew the answers, so I studied hard and my hand was always in the air. Same! I had a skill for discerning what people wanted to hear from me, and I made sure they heard it. Same! I was raised in Ronald Reagan's hometown, so I voted Republican. Same! I listened to Paul Simon, but my friends listened to Pearl Jam, so I traded "The Sound of Silence" for the loudness of grunge. Same! My dad was a therapist, so I became a therapist too. Same!

I was becoming a psychologist and a husband and a father.

But mostly, I was becoming a chameleon.

I used to be ashamed of the way I shifted colors. It seemed pathetic. Now, I know it was just my way of trying to become unlonely, and I know I'm not alone in my penchant for color-shifting. It's what we do to manufacture belonging. We hide, or more precisely, we *blend*. And it is our ego walls we hide behind, because they make great camouflage. If the people in our life are essentially unpleasant—school bullies and abusive parents, for instance—our true self will hunker down behind our ego walls and try not to make a peep. We internalize our pain, turn silence and withdrawal into an art form, and try to fly completely under the radar.

But just as often we hide in plain sight, behind our ego.

When we sense the people we want to belong to can be pleased and appeased, we try to keep them happy in order to keep them close. We build our ego wall and adorn the outside of it with mirrors, so when people look at us, they just see themselves. Same! It's a deception, of course. But the real problem is, once you've become a chameleon, it gets more and more difficult to let your true colors be seen.

A college kid is sitting in my office.

He is wise beyond his years and he's telling me about the previous night, when he was sitting around a bonfire with his closest friends, talking about philosophy and God and the universe. He said it felt like there was a wall around him, and a wall around everyone else in the circle. He said their ideas and intellects were like thick, unspoken barriers between each of them.

He felt so lonely he had to leave so he could be alone.

I asked him if there was anyone in his life he *didn't* feel lonely around—anyone who wasn't hidden by a big, thick ego wall. I was hoping he could identify at least one friend, or a mentor, or even God. I figured he'd struggle with the question and be slow to respond. I was wrong.

He looked at me with a glint in his eye and immediately said, "The kids that come into the coffee shop where I work. The young ones. Five to ten years old. Old enough to speak but not old enough to have learned they *shouldn't* speak. One day this kid was watching me make espresso, and he just blurted out, 'How does that work?' How many adults have wondered that and not asked because they were afraid of looking stupid? And the other day, I was clearing off the dessert shelf, getting ready to throw away the old pastries, and a little kid asked me if he could have one. I was about to give it to him when his mom yanked him out of the restaurant. She told him to stop acting rude."

The glint in his eye became a liquid shimmer.

"And then yesterday, this kid was sitting at the counter. He obviously had leukemia or something. He was mostly bald with wispy patches of hair all over his head. And he looked at me and he just asked me, 'Do you need any help?' This kid is sick, and he's wondering if *I* need help.

"Yeah, I don't feel lonely around those kids."

Maybe you know this story: people are bringing children to Jesus, and his closest followers rebuke him for letting it happen. Jesus responds by saying, "Let the little children come to me, and do not hinder them, for the kingdom of heaven belongs to such as these." In a way, his proclamation seems like a tease. Is Jesus giving us a clue about how to get into heaven and, if so, isn't it a little cruel to be so vague? And why does the kingdom of heaven belong to children?

I wonder if Jesus knew what my client knows.

I wonder if Jesus knew that childhood is best understood as the time before we begin to build our ego walls. I wonder if Jesus was saying that to be childlike is to be yourself, without concern for pleasing anyone or hiding anything about the good thing you are. And I wonder if Jesus was saying that's what heaven *feels* like—the freedom to be seen, to be known, and to bid farewell to the loneliness wrought by our hiding.

Maybe, in part, Jesus said the kingdom of heaven is near because heaven is present anytime two people take down the ego walls between them, drop the facades which hide them and separate them, and finally reach out and embrace the differences between them. Maybe heaven is when two or more gather and they don't declare, "Same!" Maybe heaven is when two or more gather and proclaim:

Different! But one.

Different! But united.

Different! But together.

Shortly after I watched Aidan hide himself behind a drawing he thought would please his teacher, I was flipping through his school composition book and found a poem he had written a year earlier, in fourth grade. It went like this:

> *In my poems . . .*
> *I am young and free,*
> *Back when I had no responsibility.*
> *I can write about whatever I want,*
> *Whenever I want.*
> *In my poems . . .*
> *I am a young and reckless eagle.*
> *I do whatever I want,*
> *Whenever I want.*
> *In my poems . . .*
> *I can express my feelings freely,*
> *Without getting into trouble.*
> *In my poems . . .*
> *I am one with my beautiful world,*
> *Taking what I see and putting it into words.*
> *In my poems . . .*
> *I am ME.*

Maybe the kingdom of heaven is like a poem in which we can be our truest self and still be truly one with our people. Maybe that kind of heaven *is* actually among us, and maybe we can enter it *now*. I feel like I'm starting to. These days, I still tell jokes, but only when I want to. I've realized I'm an introvert, so I rarely raise my hand in groups anymore. I tell people what I most deeply believe, instead of what they want to hear. In the voting booth, I no longer toe any party line. I love folk music—the quieter the better. I'm still a therapist, but I've discovered my own reasons for being one.

And some days, that feels almost heavenly.

This is what your soul wants to do: it wants to be itself, and then cultivate relationships and communities of belonging in which everyone else gets to be themselves too, in which everyone gets to draw what they most deeply desire to draw (even if the teacher doesn't like it), in which everyone is free to listen to their own kind of music, until the freedom to be who they are *becomes* a kind of music.

Many voices made into one chorus,

each one singing the same song of love

in their own unique and childlike voice.

CHAPTER 19

The One Sentence That Can Disarm Any Bully

It ain't what they call you, it's what you answer to.

W. C. FIELDS

In Aidan's elementary school lunchroom, there was a table of shame.

They called it "the grounded table." If a student broke a lunchroom rule, they were sent there to eat alone in silence and isolation, in front of their peers. And when their peers vacated the lunchroom for recess, they had to remain at the table and sit there alone for the entire subsequent lunch period of older students.

Like a sad animal behind the bars at a zoo.

I found out about the table on a Sunday night in Aidan's fourth-grade year, when I found him in tears. He confessed that on the previous Friday he'd gotten too loud at lunch and been sent to the grounded table. He said it was humiliating, and he was afraid of ending up there again on Monday.

It was late and I was looking for shortcuts, so I quickly began to shuffle through my bag of psychologist tricks. First, I challenged the accuracy of his perceptions, suggesting the other kids were probably too busy eating to pay attention to him. Admittedly, this was a weak start. He looked at me like I was crazy. So I switched my focus to his identity, telling him he's still a lovely boy and a good kid, no matter where the teachers make him to sit. A hint of panic entered his eyes, as if to say, "Oh no, is this the best he can do?" I tried affirming his place in the world, reminding him he was still loved by his mother and me, no matter what happened in the lunchroom. Now he looked angry, because I was obviously torturing him with crummy counseling.

None of my therapist tricks were working.

And to be honest, beneath my late-night fatigue, I was a little angry too. The lunchroom aides—good people, I'm sure, generously volunteering their time in the chaos of a grade school cafeteria—had unwittingly humiliated him, this kid I love with a fierceness that startles me sometimes. The little one in me who'd been publicly shamed about his weight in a middle school cafeteria knew exactly how Aidan felt, and I wanted to put an end to his humiliation. But I was at a loss. They were adults. Authority. Elders requiring respect.

How do you respond to shame and humiliation when you can't fight back?

Our ego is responsible for hiding us, but it's also in charge of *fighting* for us.

In graduate school, I studied marital conflict and learned that one of the most-used phrases in marital research is "negative escalation." It refers to the tit-for-tat reciprocity of animosity—the way we always up the ante in the game of aggression. I wish I had known then what I know now: negative escalation is always the result of conflict between egos.

When our ego walls fail to adequately protect us—when shame

finds its way into us once again—we add cannons to our ego walls. And basically they have one job: to pass our shame on to someone else. To discharge our pain by firing it into somebody who isn't us. To *do* hurt so we don't have to *feel* hurt. To make someone else feel smaller so we can feel bigger. Negative escalation is what happens when two egos are armed with fully loaded cannons and prepared to fight to the death.

It takes two egos to tango.

Of course, some relationships aren't characterized by negative escalation. Sometimes, a stronger ego finds a weaker ego on which to prey, someone whose ego cannons are less powerful or absent altogether, someone who doesn't have the firepower to escalate in return. The person with the weaker ego becomes the regular recipient of the shame being jettisoned by the stronger ego. In other words, sometimes when someone shames us, we don't escalate it; we *absorb* it. We take it in and it becomes a part of us. So on a Sunday evening, I wondered, *Do I encourage Aidan's little ego and his negative escalation, or do I tell him to resign himself to the shame of the grounded table?*

Are the only two responses to shame a showdown or a beat down?

I was considering telling Aidan to punch the lunchroom aide in the nose, when I remembered a story I'd heard the week before. In a nearby school district, the year had begun with lots of conflict between students, so a teacher had gathered her class together and told the kids each of their hearts was like a bucket. She told them some people would put good things in their bucket, and some people would try to put bad things in; but they should only let people put good things in their bucket. When I first heard the story, I had to chuckle, because I imagined thirty kids running to the teacher,

screaming, "Johnny just tried to put something bad in my bucket!"
But the teacher's advice hadn't ended there. She also told them this:
If anyone tries to put something bad in your bucket, *close your lid.*

Close your lid.

It reminded me of the first time I closed my lid. I had been
risking vulnerability with someone about an insecurity of mine—
showing them my soul—and they hit me where they knew it hurt
most, shaming me about my parenting. But for the first time in my
life, rather than feeling the full force of their ego cannons, I heard
the voice of grace speak up within me, whispering with a tenderness
I could hardly fathom at the time: *Sorry, the shame bank is closed.
We're not taking any more deposits today.* I didn't return the shame.
Or absorb it.

The ego angrily flips its lid, but the soul calmly *closes* it.

That Sunday night, as I ran out of psychologist tricks, I quit trying
to coach Aidan's head, and I started coaching his heart: "Bud, if they
tell you to go to the grounded table again, I want you to look them
in the eye, and I want you to say this: 'With all due respect, you can't
do that to my heart. Please send me to the principal's office instead.'"

The words startled him.

"Really," he asked, "I can *say* that?" I assured him he could, as
long as he did it with equal parts love for the big person in front of
him and the little one inside of him. His sadness and panic and anger
were replaced by a tiny smile, and he rolled over into a sound sleep.
In the end, he never needed to use the line I gave him.

He just needed to know it was okay to close his lid.

A few weeks later, in the very same cafeteria, Aidan was bullied for the first time. He was being called "four-eyes" and "nerd" and made to feel like a second-class citizen in a world full of emerging jocks and athletes. We were debriefing again, though this time he wasn't in tears, because this time the shame wasn't getting all the way into his heart. Suddenly, I wasn't so angry about the table of shame. In fact, I was a little grateful for it, because the resilience he'd learned in that moment had prepared him for this moment. Yet Aidan wasn't entirely sure how to respond, either. So I suggested the one sentence with the power to disarm almost any bully: "I like myself, and I forgive you for not liking yourself and trying to pass it on to me."

This time he laughed at me. "Dad," he said, "they're not psychologists—they're fourth graders. They're not going to under-stand that." I laughed too. Good point. But, I told him, the words weren't really for the bullies; the words were for him. The words were a reminder to him of what can happen in your heart when you close the lid and shelter yourself from shame. Then, in the space where more shame would have been deposited, there is space for something else. Love has room to get larger.

Grace has room to grow into forgiveness.

When we are responding from our pain and responding with our protective ego, forgiveness can feel impossible, almost superhuman. But with the lid of our heart closed, we can take a breath, listen for grace, and see once again *with* grace. Then, we don't see the bully's combative ego; instead, we see the wounded soul from which the bullying arises. Then, rather than focusing on all the damaging fires their ego has started, we focus on the guttering spark in their soul. Then, naturally and gradually, forgiveness takes form within us. It might take months, years, even decades. Yet when we can see even our bullies with grace, the shame they are trying to pass on to us is eventually replaced by compassion for the pain out of which their bullying arises.

When we see gracefully, loathing loses and love wins.

What does all of this have to do with belonging? Closing the lid is a prerequisite for true belonging, because we are going to have to, from time to time, forgive the ego cannons of the people we love. At some point, they will inevitably give in to the urge to pass their shame on to us, and when they do, we will need to trade in the negative escalation of our egos for the positive escalation of our souls, which looks a lot like grace and feels a lot like forgiveness.

Our bullies prepare us for our belonging.

"It's not what they call you," comedian W. C. Fields once said, "it's what you answer to." May you increasingly answer to the whisper of grace. It's inviting you to close your lid instead of taking on more shame, to create space within you instead of creating violence around you, and to let forgiveness become the durable foundation upon which an enduring belonging can be built.

— CHAPTER 20 —

The Most Painful Part of Finding Belonging

I used to think the worst thing in life was to end up alone. It's not. The worst thing in life is to end up with people who make you feel alone.

ROBIN WILLIAMS

I used to have this best friend.

We grew up in the same neighborhood, went to the same grade school, and attended the same church. We did everything together—rode bikes with banana seats all over the neighborhood, played home run derby with old tennis balls, told dirty jokes we didn't understand, and pointed flashlights in people's windows after dark. He was at our house all the time.

He was like a member of our family.

We waited together at the bus stop on our first day of middle school, studied together, tried not to get beat up together, and gave in to peer pressure too many times to count. We started dating at the same time, and when it was time to pick a college, we chose the University of Illinois. We were inseparable. But, eventually, I had to end the relationship.

Because there was another side of him.

After we hung out with other people, I'd have a pretty good feeling about how it went, but then he would start analyzing every little thing I'd done and said. It was subtle at first. If I complimented someone on their appearance, he'd wonder if it came off as creepy. If I talked about something I was proud of, he'd wonder if it came off as arrogant. And if I kept quiet, he'd wonder if it came off as snobby, disinterested, or just plain rude.

I'd end up convinced I was never going to be invited back.

I put up with it for a long time because I figured he cared about me and was just trying to protect me. Eventually, though, enough people invited me back to make me think he might be completely wrong about me. So I started speaking up. I told him I thought people invited me places because they actually wanted to be with me.

The more I pushed back, the nastier he became.

He told me I was small and I should quit acting so big. He told me I was a fraud and people wouldn't be fooled forever. By then, I barely recognized the guy he was describing, but he told me I was disloyal to disagree with him, because we were like family, and family sticks together. I kept reconciling with him and hanging out with him, because we were like blood brothers, and you don't walk out on blood, right? Yet I felt utterly alone when I was with him.

So I went looking for another way.

One day I came across a quote by an author named Lewis B. Smedes that changed things forever: "It takes one person to forgive, it takes two people to be reunited." He was talking about the difference between forgiveness and reconciliation, and essentially he was saying forgiveness is always healthy, but reconciliation is not necessarily so. If the person who is wounding us refuses to quit wounding us, then by all means forgive them—this frees us from the ongoing emotional consequences of the relationship—but for heaven's sake do not reconcile with them. That isn't good for you. It isn't good for them. It's not healthy. And it's not holy.

After I read that quote, I knew I needed to end the relationship for good. I had forgiven him many times, and I had reconciled with him too many times. So I spent time breaking up with him, telling him I forgave him but I would no longer reconcile with him.

Here's the thing, though: all those years, *my best friend wasn't an actual person.*

My best friend was my *shame*. During our backstory, shame is our nearest and dearest friend—it goes everywhere with us. Then, during our first act, we spend some time breaking up with our shame. It is the first relationship we have to end on the way to becoming unlonely. But it isn't the last. Breaking up with the shame inside of us is practice for our second act, in which we will break up with the real, live, shaming people around us. In other words, unfortunately, belonging rarely begins by adding people; it usually begins by subtracting them.

Belonging usually begins by letting go of the relationships that are most toxic to us—the ones in which we are seen as something less than we are—because when someone can't see the goodness in us, it doesn't mean they're bad, but it does mean they're bad *for us*. We can't change anyone's opinion of us, because we can't convince anyone to see us differently—we can only give them opportunities to change and chances to see us for who we really are. However, when they don't or won't or can't, the thing we *can* control is what we do with the relationship.

So, we may have to let go of lifelong friendships. We may have to quit a job, and the colleagues and bosses who go with it. We may have to get free of toxic family members—the ones who, for whatever reason, refuse to see us for the good soul we are. We may even face tough decisions about spouses who abuse us with their shaming and multiply our loneliness with their low opinion of us.

Of course, such decisions are best made in consultation with wise counsel. It is essential to solicit the feedback of someone we trust to tell us the truth, because it is possible the feelings we are experiencing are still arising from the shame inside of us rather than the people around us. Furthermore, if we do ultimately decide to end a toxic relationship, it is important to have someone hold us accountable for ending it with as much integrity as possible.

This is *exquisitely* painful stuff.

And perhaps the most painful part is allowing the people we love to keep their hurtful opinions about us. If we don't, we will remain fused to them by our desire to convince them of our goodness. We have to accept there are people who don't think much of us, who dislike us, who see us in ways we are not. And we have to *let* them be wrong about us. This is how we move away from the people who leave us lonely and create space for the people to whom we'll eventually belong. Usually, our circles must shrink before they can expand.

The losses can be so profound it may feel as if all is lost.

Usually, near the end of the second act of a story, the protagonist experiences the most devastating setback in the tale. It's the all-is-lost moment, the moment of despair, the moment in which it seems certain the character we've come to love will meet his or her demise. In the story of our lives, the dwindling of our crowd can feel like that moment, because in that moment, there is no guarantee the crowd won't dwindle all the way to zero.

But it won't.

If we are willing to go through this painful moment of our

story, if we choose to love ourselves bravely by letting go of those who don't love us, if we choose not to give in to the despair, if we begin to invest our time and energy into moments and relationships and communities of people who sincerely want to embrace what we've already embraced about ourselves, it won't end in loneliness. Instead, by vulnerably announcing who we are and waiting to see who rejoices at the announcement, we will gradually begin to find— and trust—the people to whom we truly belong.

To be clear, this is not about gathering around us groups of people who go to the same church or vote for the same candidate. This is about attracting to us people who have also broken up with their best friend called shame; people who have discovered the beauty they possess and want to give it away like the gift it is; people who know they are lonely and simply want to share their loneliness with us rather than expecting us to fix it; people who have peered into the depths of love and life and want to plumb them; people who have begun to believe grace is not a fairy tale.

People who have begun to believe grace is the greatest story ever told.

Though it's been a number of years since I broke up with my best friend, shame, I've continued to hear his voice in the voices of other people. Sometimes that voice is merely a projection—the dwindling echo of the shame inside of me, to which I was once so close—but at other times, the shame I've heard in the voices of other people has been quite real. Some of those people have been friends. Some of them family. Sometimes I hear shame's voice in the comments of people on the Internet, who read my writing and tell me how clueless I am, how much damage I do with my opinions, and how doomed my children will be as a result. It's been awfully tempting to waste a lot of time and energy trying to convince them I'm not such a bad guy. But instead, I try to remind myself I don't need to be in relationship with all people, and I certainly can't make everyone like me or believe in me. And then I break up with my best friend all over again. Sometimes that means putting a little extra distance in a relationship.

Sometimes it means walking away altogether.

I'd be surprised if you don't already have someone coming to mind—perhaps even several someones—a person or people you truly love but who, it seems, will never be able to love you for who you truly are. You may even be thinking of someone who has been in your life since you were a little one. The winnowing will be painful but necessary, because in the end, your energy will be freed up for your relationships with the people who *have* responded joyfully to your announcement about who you are. And when those people wound you—as they inevitably will, because they're human—you will want to forgive them *and* reconcile with them. Then, though you may not watch your circles of belonging expand, there will be great joy in watching them *deepen.*

Your place of true belonging will be like a small pool,

in a quiet forest,

with cool waters,

and a bottom too deep to touch.

CHAPTER 21

When Announcing Yourself Means Announcing Your Need

Friends show their love in times
of trouble, not in happiness.

EURIPIDES

*I*t's the day I've been waiting for.

My wife and I are flying from Chicago to Denver for a convention, and after we arrive, I'll be joining a conference call with my literary agent and a major publishing house. It's my first meeting with an editor to discuss the possibility of writing my first book. It could be my big break—you know, the one that will solve all my problems and make my life perfect. I can't remember the last time I felt so anxious. I want it to go flawlessly. So I've given myself plenty of time before the call to retrieve luggage, catch a shuttle to the hotel, and settle into the room.

But then the storms hit—literally.

We're about to board our plane when the flight attendant announces that another line of summer thunderstorms is rolling through Chicago and the flight will be delayed thirty minutes. *No problem,* I think, *we've got plenty of time. Hours even.* But then, just as we're about to board again, another delay. And then another. The new projected arrival time means I'm going to be on a loud and crowded shuttle at the time of the call. I can picture myself, finger pressed against my ear, asking repeatedly, "Can you hear me now?" while the editor fumes and kicks herself for scheduling a meeting with this rookie.

I tend to function as a Lone Ranger. I take care of myself, pull myself up by my bootstraps, and don't expect help from anyone. My wife, though, has always had a knack for building community. She attracts the same robust kind of love she gives. She leans on the people who lean on her. In other words, she's good at belonging. So as I'm panicking about my doomed interview, my wife is doing something else.

She's picking up the phone.

When we bid farewell to the people who won't or can't see the light inside of us, our world becomes a lot less populated. The people who'd been hanging around because they could push us around eventually go away. And who is left? The people we can call on when the storms hit. Our numbers dwindle but, ironically, our loneliness does too, because we find ourselves surrounded by a small band of brothers or sisters who have our back.

Seventeenth-century poet and cleric John Donne first said, "No man is an island," and Thomas Merton popularized the saying in the twentieth century. Life is a train wreck. Mess is inevitable. Bad stuff happens. It just does. It's not a cosmically designed punishment or life lesson. Some days the storms just roll in and wreak havoc, wrecking our plans and putting our dreams—sometimes even our life—in jeopardy. But when the storms do hit, we have an opportunity to *redeem* them. On days like that, we discover that to live from our soul—the great, powerful, divine thing at the center of us—is, paradoxically, to become aware of our dependence on *other* souls. When the bad stuff happens, it's a chance to rely on the *good* stuff in other people.

And the people who bring the good stuff are the people we belong to.

My wife picks up the phone and calls a friend who arrived at the convention a day earlier. Like an advance scout, he tells us the hotel is almost forty-five minutes outside of Denver and the shuttle will never get us there in time for the interview. But then he tells us he rented a car the day before, he'll be parked at the curb when we arrive, and he'll break the speed limit to get us to the hotel on time.

We land in Denver and, as promised, he's waiting at the curb. It looks like we'll make it in the nick of time. However, after a day of travel, my phone is almost dead. I'm going to get to the hotel on time, but I won't have a way to reach the publisher. My friend reaches into the glove compartment and pulls out a phone charger with an adapter for every phone ever invented. I plug in my phone, and he hits the accelerator.

The people we belong to charge us up when it feels like we're going dead. They respond with what we need in our time of need. They show up when the storms blow in. And they do so not because they are expecting to get something in return. When we ask for help, there are no questions asked. The people we belong to are filled with grace and spill it wherever they go. And one place they've committed to go is *toward* us.

Even when it means driving into the storm to get us.

I walk into our hotel room with three minutes to spare. I try to breathe slowly, and I call in at the appointed time. The interview is not a smashing success, but it's not a total failure either. It's somewhere in the middle, like most of life. The call ends and I put down my phone, but as soon as I do, it rings again.

My personal storm may have passed, but the storms in Chicago haven't.

My mother-in-law is watching our kids for the weekend, juggling all their activities, and evacuating our house every few hours so realtors can show it and hopefully sell it. Meanwhile, the summer thunderstorms have continued to intensify. Then, around the time my oldest son spikes a high fever, the thunderstorms start *spinning*—a tornado touches down sixty miles away. My mother-in-law is in way over her head. But the phone calls from home are not from her.

They're from friends.

Friends who, without being asked, are stepping into the storm for us. They're taking our youngest two kids for the night and offering a place of shelter as the weather system passes, and more than anything, they're offering my mother-in-law the greatest reassurance of all: *You are not alone.* She, too, apparently, without even asking, belongs to the people we belong to.

Sometimes, the people we belong to are watching so closely, they know our need before we're even aware of it. That kind of love and attention can be a little unsettling when you're used to living like a Lone Ranger. But when God shows up looking like a whole neighborhood of people who are loving you as well as you've ever been loved in your life, well, it's best not to fight back against the many loving hands of grace.

It's best just to let them hold you up when the wind is blowing you down.

Two days later, we're still in Colorado, the storms back home have mostly passed, and I'm standing at the edge of the Continental Divide with my wife and our friends who'd met us with the car and the phone charger and the saving grace. We've hiked for two strenuous hours up steep, winding paths, and we've arrived at our destination—a lookout from which you can see the Rockies sprawling in every direction.

But I'm huddled, hiding, inside a grove of trees.

I'm terrified of heights and my terror is multiplied by open spaces. This is my worst nightmare. We've climbed all this way to reach this glorious height, and I'm too scared to step out of the safety of the trees toward the edge of the cliff.

As I hunker down in the trees, though, I'm overwhelmed by the metaphor: I'm hiding in the trees all alone and the world is out there and it's brilliant and it's beautiful. My friends are out there—grace in hiking boots—inviting me into it, coaxing me from my safe place, reassuring me they'll be there with me and telling me it's breathtaking but safe and we'll do it together. Sometimes a metaphor is enough—I decide if I can trust my people with my conference call and my kids and my house, then I can certainly trust them to be there for me on a rocky cliff.

So I step out.

This is what true belonging has the power to do—it can give you the courage to step out. To take risks. To venture into your discomfort zone. To try new things. To be a little dangerous. In a word, to *live*. Because you know you're not alone. You know you're safe in the best sense of the word—the storms may come but you'll have a shelter to run to, or even better, a shelter that will run to *you*.

Surely you have cliffs in your life—places and paths and

moments and opportunities that are both terrifying and beautiful in their potential. Surrounded by the people you belong to, you will be invited out onto your cliff. If you dare, you will timidly but courageously approach the edge.

And you may even begin to see, sprawling out before you, what you're here to do.

CHAPTER 22

Why Belonging Is Another Beginning

A friend is a loved one who awakens your life in
order to free the wild possibilities within you.

JOHN O'DONOHUE

*f*ifteen years ago today, I proposed to my wife.

She committed herself to me that day, and in the last fifteen laps around the sun, she has committed to me again and again. She committed in front of a justice of the peace when we signed our marriage license. She committed in front of our family and friends on our wedding day. Three times she has committed to raising a child with me. And 5,475 times she has committed to faithfulness and fidelity—every morning upon waking. Then, last summer, in a dimly lit winery at the edge of Chicago, while listening to a little-known folk-rock band, she made one more commitment to me, and it changed everything. With ten words, she awakened my life and called forth the wild possibilities within me. In other words, she made the kind of commitment that is the bedrock of belonging.

I've always been a researcher of belonging.

As an undergrad, I began studying a specific kind of belonging called marriage. I continued my research in grad school, wrote a master's thesis, conducted a dissertation study, and have seen hundreds of couples in marital therapy over the last decade. In my practice, I've encountered everything I studied in the lab: the disappointed realism following wedding day idealism, communication catastrophes, the minefield of co-parenting, and gut-wrenching infidelity, to name just a few. But I've also encountered a surprisingly large subset of couples I'd never heard of before. No one studies them. No one talks about them. And no one knows how to help them.

These couples function pretty well together. For the most part, they speak kindly to each other, respect each other as people, care for each other as partners, run a family efficiently, and make enough money to get by. They can't point to any glaring problems in their marriage, and yet they are utterly dissatisfied with it. Over time, they slowly become disillusioned with the whole enterprise, because they are living a textbook marriage and yet can't find the fulfillment it was supposed to bring them. Admittedly, for many years, I didn't know how to help these couples either. Until I realized what was vexing me so much in my *own* marriage.

I had made my marriage the purpose of my life.

The couples in my office weren't dissatisfied and disillusioned because they were doing anything wrong in their marriages; they were disappointed because they had expected the wrong thing *from* their marriages—they had expected marriage to completely satisfy their need for a purpose. In the first act of our lives, we learned that no marriage, relationship, or community can bear the weight of our search for worthiness. If we are to enter the third act of our lives, we must embrace the remainder of the truth: our places of belonging cannot bear the weight of our search for *purpose*, either. Our places of belonging are meant for something else.

They are meant to free the wild possibilities within us.

Last summer, my wife and I fought rush hour traffic to arrive early for the concert at the winery on the edge of Chicago, because we were determined not to miss the headliner—one of our favorite musicians. As we sipped wine and ate appetizers, the opening band took the stage. Two young guys. A guitar. A cello. Folk music with a twist. They were surprisingly good. Though, as I watched them under the hot lights, making their art in front of a small roomful of people, it wasn't the quality of their music that moved me.

It was the quality of their determination.

It was their dedication to translating the abstract passion of their hearts into tangible art. It was the determination not to die with their souls trapped quietly inside them. It was the abandon with which they threw themselves into their creative expression. They were almost half my age, but suddenly I wanted to be like them when I grew up.

By that time, I'd been blogging weekly for three years, struggling to write a book proposal for a year, and doing all of it amid my full-time job, family obligations, and a life so full it pushed everything passionate to the narrow margins. The book was what fanned the embers of the spark within me, but there was no time to write it. I wanted to be like those young musicians. I wanted to let my words out and put them under the bright lights. I needed them not to be hidden inside me anymore, because trapped passions are painful, like an infected splinter under the skin. I wanted to stand up and make my art. Take a risk with it. Maybe crash and burn, but at least try to get it off the ground. As I watched them, I had tears in my eyes, but they weren't tears of inspiration.

They were tears of desperation.

I saw no way to live out my dream. My circumstances just wouldn't allow it. I was trapped within my debts and obligations. I was caught up in patterns and routines that seemed completely intractable. As tears sprang to my eyes, my wife grabbed my hand, turned to me, her own eyes glittering with tears, and gave me her ten-word commitment: "We're going to change our life. So you can write."

Freud said our nighttime dreams represent our deepest wishes. Our *daydreams* do too. A daydream is simply a passion unlived. It is the soul slumbering. On the other hand, a passion lived is our soul coming fully awake by doing what it has always wanted to do in the world. In other words, our dreams are not the things we can't do or the things we don't know how to do; they are almost always the things we deeply *desire* to do but simply *aren't* doing. When we start doing them, they cease to be dreams and they become our passions.

Your place of belonging is where you're encouraged to turn your dream into your passion.

It took 351 days to change our life.

During that year, my wife began to remember some of her own dreams. She'd begun her education with a desire to provide psycho-logical services to kids and families who cannot typically afford such services. Instead, she became a tenured and decorated professor of psychology, teaching about therapy but not actually providing it. She loved what she was doing. It was in the neighborhood of her deepest desire.

But she wanted to live her passion and wake up completely.

So when she got an unsolicited job offer from a pediatric development center in the small, rural, and mostly impoverished town where I grew up, it was my turn to commit to *her*. It was my turn to show her the kind of belonging that insists on turning a dream into a passion. We put our house on the market and started looking for a house in my hometown. But really, we had already found the home we were looking for, because home is the place of belonging where someone loves you enough to fan the flames of the spark that has always been alight at the center of you.

Almost one year after the concert that changed our life, we moved back to my boyhood hometown, where my wife could work the job she had always wanted to work, and I could write the book I had always wanted to write. I think that's what true belonging does, whether we find it in marriage or friendship or any other form of committed community. It invites us to be the people we're here to be and to do the things we're here to do. Which is why belonging is never the end of our story. It's more like the voice of grace, uttered on the tongues of our people.

Inviting us into the third act of our life.

A Father's Letter to His Son
(about the Only Good Reason to Get Married)

Dear Son,

It seems like yesterday you were blowing poop out of your diaper onto your mother's lap. I blinked, and now you're on the verge of birds and bees and *dating*. The poop was a lot simpler. Yet I think we can simplify relationships by talking about marriage and then working backward. Because if you understand the only good reason to get married, it can make sense of everything else as well.

Buddy, you're going to want to get married for all the wrong reasons. We all do. In fact, the most common reason to get married also happens to be the most dangerous: we get married because we think it will make us happy. Getting married in order to be happy is the surest way to get divorced. There are beautiful marriages. But marriages don't become beautiful by seeking happiness; they become beautiful by seeking something *else*. Marriages become beautiful when two people embrace the only good reason to get married: to practice the daily sacrifice of their egos.

Ego.

You may be hearing that word for the first time. It probably sounds foreign and confusing to you. This is what it means to me:

Your ego is the part of you that protects your heart. You were born with a good and beautiful heart, and it will never leave you. But when I was too harsh toward you or your friends made fun of your extracurricular choices or you made a mistake, you started to doubt if your heart was good enough to belong. Don't worry, it happens to all of us at some point.

And so your mind began to build a wall around your heart. That happens to all of us too. It's like a big castle wall with a huge moat—it keeps us safe from invaders who might want to get in and attack our heart. And thank goodness for your ego wall! Your heart is worthy of protection, buddy.

At first, we only use the ego wall to keep people out. But eventually, as we grow up, we get tired of hiding fearfully and decide the best defense is a good offense. We put cannons on our ego wall and we start firing. For some people that looks like anger. For other people it looks like gossip and judgment and divisiveness.

Eventually, many of us realize our cannons have backfired and are only making us lonelier, so we build an ego throne—a place of perfection in which we expect to be respected. On my ego throne, I pretend everyone on the outside of my walls is wrong. It makes me feel right and righteous, but really it just keeps me perched safely atop my ideas.

Buddy, I know I've fired my ego cannons at you from time to time, and I know I have a bad habit of looking down upon you from my throne, and for that I'm truly sorry. Sometimes we need our egos to survive.

Most of the time we don't.

Most of the time, our egos ruin any chance we might have of finding a place to belong, including an enduringly joyful marriage. Because, in the end, the entire purpose of marriage is to step down from your ego throne, disarm your ego cannons, and to step out from behind your ego wall. Until you are fully available to the person you love. Open. Vulnerable.

Dangerously united.

Many people are going to tell you the key to a happy marriage is to put God at the center of it, but I think it depends on what your experience of God does for your ego. Because if your God is one of strength and power and domination, a God who proves you're always right and creates dividing lines by which you judge everyone else, a God who keeps you safe and secure, I think you should keep that God as far from the center of your marriage as you can.

He'll only build your ego wall taller and stronger.

But if the God you experience is a vulnerable one, a God who turns the world upside down and dwells in the midst of brokenness and embraces everyone on the margins and will sacrifice anything for peace and reconciliation and wants to trade safety and security for a dangerous and risky love, then I agree, put him right at the center of your marriage. If your God is in the business of ego surrender, he will transform your marriage into sacred ground.

What's the secret to a happy marriage?

Marry someone who has also embraced the only good reason to get married.

Someone who will commit to dying alongside you—not in fifty years, but daily, as they surrender their ego with you. Someone who will be more faithful to you than they are to their own safety. Someone willing to embrace the beauty of sacrifice, the yielding of their strength, and the peril of vulnerability. Someone willing to thread their dreams and passions into yours and weave together the fabric of a life with as few regrets as you can manage. In other words, someone who wants to spend their one life stepping into a crazy, dangerous love with you and only you.

With my walls down,

Dad

—— *Act Three*: *Purpose* ——

*Everyone has been made for some
particular work, and the desire for that
work has been put in every heart.*

RUMI

Words from a Father to His Daughter
(from the Makeup Aisle)

Dear Little One,

As I write this, I'm sitting in the makeup aisle of our local Target store. A friend recently texted me from a different makeup aisle and told me it felt like one of the most oppressive places in the world. I wanted to find out what he meant. And now that I'm sitting here, I'm beginning to agree with him. Words have *power*, and the words on display in this aisle have a *deep* power. Words and phrases like:

Affordably gorgeous,

Infallible,

Flawless finish,

Brilliant strength,

Liquid power,

Go nude,

Age defying,

Instant age rewind,

Choose your dream,

Nearly naked, and

Natural beauty.

When you have a daughter, you start to realize she's as strong as everyone else in the house—a force to be reckoned with, a soul on fire with the same life and gifts and passions as any man. But sitting in this store aisle, you also begin to realize most people won't see her that way. They'll see her as a pretty face and a body to enjoy. And they'll tell her she has to look a certain way to have any worth or influence.

But words *do* have power, and maybe, just maybe, the words of a father can begin to compete with the words of the world. Maybe a father's words can deliver his daughter through this gauntlet of institutionalized shame and into a deep, unshakeable sense of her own worthiness and beauty.

Little One, a father's words aren't different words, but they are words with a radically different *meaning*:

Brilliant strength. May your strength be not in your *fingernails* but in your *heart*. May you discern in your center who you are, and then may you fearfully but tenaciously live it out in the world.

Choose your dream. But not from a department store shelf. Find the still-quiet place within you. A real dream has been planted there. Discover what you want to do in the world. And when you have chosen, may you faithfully pursue it with integrity and with hope.

Naked. The world wants you to take your clothes off. Please keep them on. But take your *gloves* off. Pull no punches. Say what is in your heart. Be vulnerable. Embrace risk. Love a world that barely knows what it means to love itself. Do so nakedly. Openly. With abandon.

Infallible. May you be constantly, infallibly aware that infallibility doesn't *exist*. It's an illusion created by people interested in your wallet. If you choose to seek perfection, may it be in an infallible *grace*—for yourself, and for everyone around you.

Age defying. Your skin will wrinkle and your youth will fade, but your *soul* is ageless. It will always know how to play and how to enjoy and how to revel in this one-chance life. May you always defiantly resist the aging of your *spirit*.

Flawless finish. Your finish has nothing to do with how your *face* looks today and everything to do with how your *life* looks on your *last* day. May your years be a preparation for that day. May you be aged by grace, may you grow in wisdom, may your love become big enough to embrace all people, and may your joy have no bottom. May your flawless finish be a peaceful embrace of the end and the unknown that follows, and may it thus be a gift to everyone who cherishes you.

Little One, you love everything pink and frilly and I will surely understand if someday makeup is important to you. But I pray three words will remain *more* important to you—the last three words you say every night, when I ask the question, "Where are you the most beautiful?" Three words so bright no concealer can cover them.

Where are you the most beautiful?

On the inside.

Love,

Daddy

CHAPTER 23

The Thing You Never Knew You Always Wanted to Do

*If tomorrow morning, by some stroke of magic every
dazed and benighted soul woke up with the power to
take the first step toward pursuing his or her dreams,
every shrink in the directory would be out of business . . .
Look in your own heart. Unless I'm crazy, right now
a still, small voice is piping up, telling you as it has ten
thousand times, the calling that is yours and yours alone.*

STEVEN PRESSFIELD

Several years ago, hospice nurse Bronnie Ware posted online a list of the top regrets of her dying patients. The number one regret was this: "I wish I'd had the courage to live a life true to myself, not the life others expected of me." The list went viral. Why? Because her patients are fading echoes of the voice of grace—that still, small voice—within each of us, urging us to quit doing the things we think we *should* do with our life, and to start doing the things we *want* to do with our life.

In third grade, Aidan's teacher told us Aidan was "depressed."

I'm a psychologist, and when you use that word about my eight-year-old, warning bells go off. Aidan had begun the year with a zeal for school and schoolwork, but he'd become despondent and sullen in the classroom. I took him out for donuts and a talk, because any conversation is easier with all-you-can-eat donuts.

Two donuts in, I asked him how he was feeling about school, half expecting a blank stare or a confused look. But before the words were out of my mouth, his eyes were filled with tears, and through trembling lips he said, "It's just that God gives everyone a skill, and mine is school, and I don't want to disappoint anyone." Can a heart melt and a stomach cramp at the same time? Let me assure you, they can.

I had no idea Aidan was already listening to the voice of his shame.

What I said next made him blink hard and look at me like I was a little crazy. "I don't think God gives us our skills," I said. "I think we get our skills by accident, like we get our hair color and eye color." I wasn't trying to comfort him. I was trying to save him the confusion I witness every day in my therapy office.

Last year, this all happened in *one* day . . .

In the morning, I got a call from someone who wanted therapy because, he said, his corporate job was numbing him. He was a skilled businessman, making a bunch of money, and slowly dying right in the middle of his most profitable talents. He said he needed to stop doing what he was good at and start doing something he was in love with.

Around noon, I met with a brilliant administrator who deftly manages multiple million-dollar projects for a massive company and is quickly working his way up the ladder. Yet he sat in my office and observed, "Everyone who's happy has their something they create. I need my something." He's telling a *success* story with his life, but he wants to tell a *beautiful* story.

Around dinnertime, I met with a man who is great at what he does, so when quitting time rolls around, he rolls right through it. When I asked him what he would do if he were to quit at quitting time, his eyes got bright and he responded immediately: since childhood, he's always wanted to do woodworking. Instead, he usually chooses *over*working.

Later that night, I met a friend for drinks. He's an intellectual at the pinnacle of his profession, but, he told me, he wakes up every morning thinking about the book he wants to write, and goes to sleep thinking about it too. Some days he can think of little else.

In one day, four very skilled, very successful people reminded me of something, and I need to remind you of it too: if you get to the top by burying your passions and focusing exclusively on your most marketable skills, there's no satisfaction and no peace waiting for you at the top of your accomplishments. There's no happiness and no joy. Only the feeling of a light slowly dimming within you.

Yet, as children, we are seduced into idolizing our skills. Sometimes we're seduced by shame: our parents beam with pride when we bring home a report card with a bunch of A's or our coach tells us how important we are to next year's squad, and shame whispers, promising us we'll finally be good enough if we're good *at* something. For the most skilled among us, this promise is a carrot to chase all the way to the top, and for the less skilled, it's a verdict declaring life was over before it ever started.

Other times we get seduced by big people with big mortgages, who tell us our skills pay the bills. Writing is lovely and drawing is cute, but what are you going to do with an English major or an art degree? Major in business. Or pick a trade. Get a job. Be *stable*.

Now, please understand, stability and independence are important—I love my kids, but I don't want to still be supporting them when they're forty. Yet skill and stability aren't the *only* things that matter in life. As we age, we slowly discover our skills alone can't make us truly come alive. Nor can any of the other things we think we "should" do—all the agendas and obligations and responsibilities placed on us by people who want what's important to them to become what's urgent to us.

The third act of life—like the third act of any good story—is the part of your story in which the great dramatic question of your life finds some resolution. In life, that question is, *Why am I here?* Yet in life, resolution doesn't mean conclusion; it means *clarity*. It isn't an ending; it's a *sending*. It is where you seize the opportunity—the one that's always been in front of you, though perhaps you haven't known it—to craft a life revolving around something other than what you are *good* at doing, or what other people tell you that you *should* be doing. It's an opportunity to start listening to the voice of grace inside you and the voices of grace around you—the people you belong to—the voices who want to see you do what *you've* always wanted to do with your life. So your third act doesn't begin with a skill.

It begins with the little one inside you. Who has a passion.

Donut number two was completely forgotten and Aidan's head was cocked in an expression of immense skepticism when I said, "Maybe God doesn't give us our skills; maybe the real gift is our *passions*. Maybe our passions are knitted into us, and maybe we were meant to enjoy them and to be creative in the world through them. Buddy, what do you think is *your* passion?"

His lips had stopped trembling, and he nibbled thoughtfully on the lower one. Then those lips curled in a knowing grin, and there were pools in his eyes again, but now they were shimmering with glee. He looked at me with confidence and said, "I love to *learn*."

This time, my heart melted and my stomach *flipped*.

Aidan *does* love to learn. He is enthralled by the world and wants to know everything about how it works. He tries to ace social studies because he's good at it and he thinks he *should*, but he gets lost in his Civil War almanac because he's passionate about it, and it's what he *wants* to do. From the outside, they look a lot alike. Yet, whereas the pursuit of good grades deprives the spark within him of oxygen, the pursuit of *knowledge* fans the flame. A Civil War almanac would put me to sleep, but it wakes him up—it wakes his *soul* up.

The dictionary defines *passion* as "a strong or extravagant fondness, enthusiasm, or desire for anything." Extravagant fondness. I love the sound of that. To live passionately is to be extravagantly fond of the things we are doing in the world.

Extravagant fondness looks like the teenager who quits baseball so he can have more time to write poetry, because the lines of verse make his heart quicken. Or the kid who quits doodling in his notebook and joins the baseball team because the smell of an old leather mitt and the feel of a new leather ball make his heart pound. Or the college student who changes majors way "too late" in the game, because the psychology classes are leaving her hollow, but gazing up at the stars on that astronomy field trip last month ripped open a sense of wonder in her that she wants to live in forever. Or the middle manager who cuts back his hours so he can step into Little League coaching, because managing grown minds is mundane to him, but molding young minds is enthralling to him. Or the young woman who quits her catering job so she can clean houses every day, because a sparkling countertop is the way she wants to put her spark into the world. Or the young mother who pulls her kids out of school because her fondness for teaching cannot be tamed and she's awed by the minds of her children. Or the mother who starts sending her kids to school after years of homeschooling because the desire to be a student again has been burning inside her for over a decade and has finally shone through.

What is shining its way through all *your* shoulds?

Because something *is* shining inside of you. And despite what you may be telling yourself, you probably already know what it is.

In my office, the first lament, "I want to find my passion!" is almost always followed by a second lament, "But I don't know what it is." The first lament is always true, but the second one almost always is not. The truth is we are, all of us, already tipping in the direction of our passions.

For years, I didn't know this. When clients asked for help in identifying their passions, I dug in with them. Explored. Discussed. Processed. Problem-solved. I eventually realized, though, I was part of the problem. We already know what we want to do, and all our analysis is simply a clever, unconscious way of keeping ourselves on the fence. Making changes is scary. Trying something new is risky. Uncertainty abounds. The fence, on the other hand, is familiar. Miserable to sit on, perhaps, but *known* and thus relatively safe.

So these days, when someone tells me they don't know what their passion is, I tell them they don't need to discover what they want to do; they just need to admit it. This third act of life doesn't begin with a big leap; it begins with a big *lean*. We let ourselves tip right off the fence in the direction we want to go and let gravity pull us into a life of extravagant fondness.

I'm aware that by writing about the third act of life and the passions we discover there, I'm entering into an increasingly loud and diverse conversation about "how to find your passion." I'm choosing to enter the conversation because I'm concerned some of the voices involved are talking about passion out of order and, thus, without the proper context. In other words, without a solid foundation in worthiness and belonging, the talk of finding our passions starts to sound an awful lot like the voice of shame.

The voice of shame says our passions, if they are going to matter, must be earth-shattering or world-changing. It subtly substitutes performance for passion and then pawns it off as the real deal. So before I talk more about passion and purpose, I think it's important to undo some of the talk you've probably already heard—around you or within you—about passion.

This is what passion is not . . .

Passion is not about saving the world. In the words of author Anne Lamott, "Lighthouses don't go running all over an island looking for boats to save; they just stand there shining." Passion is about simply letting the light within you shine in the things you do. Our passions are not necessarily epic. They are not always big, world-changing things. They're just things that won't go away, things that won't leave us alone. It's as if the little one inside of us is tugging on the shirtsleeve of our hearts and won't quit tugging until we pay attention.

Passion is not about inspiring anyone else. For instance, I write. My passion is sitting alone in a room all day by myself with just a laptop and my thoughts. To many people, that would be excruciatingly mundane. But when I'm writing, I feel fully alive. In contrast, some people are passionate about exploring every corner of the earth. I don't understand them. I like my little room. But that's what awakens *them*. That's *their* passion. Our passions don't have to inspire anyone else; they just need to breathe new life into *us*.

Passion is not necessarily a career. There's an awful lot of talk about turning your passion into a paycheck—quitting your old job, finding a job you love, starting a business. If you can pull that off, great. Go for it. Yet if you do, be careful about preserving your passion, because a paycheck can turn a passion into a profession awfully quickly. It can go from opening up your soul to weighing it down. Fundamentally, your passion is not about making a living; it's about living with the eyes of your soul wide open.

Passion is not the sole possession of privileged people. Too many of us buy into the fatalistic idea that only people with enough resources and time have the freedom to practice their passion. Notice the word *enough*. It's a red flag signaling shame. Passion arises from the spark that shines equally in everyone—in men and in women, in the young and the old, in the middle-aged career person and the retiree, in the affluent and the impoverished. All of us have equal access to our passions. Whoever you are, extravagant fondness is available to you.

Right now.

I wonder what story Aidan will tell with his life if he holds on to his extravagant fondness for learning and refuses to get distracted by his skillfulness at school. I wonder what beauty he will make in this world if he does what he wants rather than what he thinks he should do. I wonder what the third act of his life will look like if he continues to honor the little one inside of him who knows *exactly* what he's passionate about doing.

And I wonder the same things about you.

What would happen if you listened to that little one again? What would happen if you let yourself lean in the direction of your passion and started doing the thing you've always wanted to do? I have a couple of guesses. I'm guessing you'd start dabbling in joy, multiplying your energies, birthing creativity, shining your light, spreading your goodness, and lavishing your love. I'm guessing you'd start putting me, the therapist, out of business.

One passionate day at a time.

— CHAPTER 24 —

The Question That Can Silence Any Story

*Don't ask what the world needs. Ask what makes
you come alive, and go do it. Because what the
world needs is people who have come alive.*

HOWARD THURMAN

I know a woman who has a story to tell.

She wants to write a novel about the day her life changed. The day she felt the lump. The day the illusion of control was ripped from her. The day she was pulled off the path she'd been walking and dropped onto a path called chemotherapy and uncertainty and fear. She looks around at a culture obsessed with violent metaphors—a culture that talks about breast cancer as if it's a war: "battling" it, "fighting" for your life—and she wants to tell the *other* side of the story. She wants to write about what it's like to sit in a chair for hours upon hours, having poison pumped into her veins while it slowly dawns on her: *There is nothing to fight.* No control to be wrested from the Fates. She wants to tell the story of jumping into that dark abyss and finding light at the bottom of it. Right now, that is her passion. But so far, she hasn't. Why? Because she's asking the question that can silence any story: Does it *matter*?

She doesn't know if people will be interested in her story. She doesn't know if it will move anybody or make a difference to anyone. And that is terrifying to her. Almost as terrifying as the cancer. Because this is *her* story. Her identity. At some level, she is, like all of us, harboring this fear: *If what I'm passionate about doing doesn't matter to anyone else, then maybe I don't matter.* So her story stays trapped inside of her.

I know how she feels.

I wrestled with the does-it-matter question after I watched *Hotel Rwanda* and was confronted with the horror of genocide. I'm passionate about redeeming the brokenness of this world—it's why I do what I do as a psychologist—but suddenly, when faced with the magnitude of genocidal brokenness, a day in my therapy office seemed pretty inconsequential. On a busy day, I help ten people through a little more of their pain. Meanwhile, halfway around the world, thousands of people are being slaughtered with machetes.

How can my work possibly matter?

The question arose again, for a while, when I first considered blogging. I looked at all the blog posts in my Facebook feed and asked what one more blog could possibly do, except add to the digital clutter. Surely, I thought, someone out there is saying it better, and to a bigger audience. And the question arose once more when it came time to write this book. I tried to begin the manuscript right after walking through a bookstore. I'd gone to the overstuffed self-help section and wondered if my book would be the straw that broke the camel's back—the tome that made the shelves finally collapse.

The question arises again and again inside each of us. We are a humanity stretched at the seams by passions swelling and ready to burst forth, by steps waiting to be taken, by stories of extravagant fondness waiting to be told. We are a people poised to unleash the light within us upon the darkness that moves among us, and yet we push back against it and stuff it back down inside us, because, really? Does my little passion matter?

And yet I can't shake the image of gnarled hands on Christmas bells.

I can't shake the image of those disabled children hobbling to the front of that sparkling auditorium. I remember them picking up the bells, barely, with twisted hands and uncooperative fingers. I remember their conductor, standing in front of them, pointing at them gently, waiting for them to play their part, to add their one note to the beauty they were all making together. I remember the audience watching in wonder, throats choked with emotion. It was as if grace, for a moment, chose to sing instead of whisper, reminding every single soul in the auditorium, it *all* matters. It's mysterious and incomprehensible, but it all matters.

And the tears in every eye testified to it.

I can't shake the image of Aidan, heart split wide open by a homeless, fingerless veteran on a street corner in Chicago. Our family walked by him, each of us shaken, but not breaking stride. Aidan's hand grasped the back of my shirt, stopping me short. His big, round eyes filled with tears.

"Please, Daddy, give me just a dollar so I can give it to him. *Please.*"

I remember him handing the bill to the man and responding to the man's thank-you by looking him in the eye and saying, "You're welcome." Does the man matter? Aidan's tears testified to it. Does what Aidan did matter? Will it change the world, end the homeless problem, fix that man's problems? No. But does it matter? You bet it matters.

My tears testifed to it.

I can't shake the image of Quinn barricading the driveway with his body, refusing to let us back up the car. He hates being late to school, but he's even more concerned for the lone worm that wandered onto the driveway during last night's thunderstorm. He's touching the wound at the center of him—the wound of a middle child who feels like he's all alone and fears nobody is watching out for him—and he's making that wound available to a creature that will never know he exists. I'm tempted to threaten him with a grounding unless he gets in the car, but the beautiful note Quinn is playing deserves an ear for the listening, so I get out and together we move the worm back to the grass.

Let's not overglorify this moment. There's no butterfly effect here. That worm isn't going to set off a series of chain reactions that will ripple through the cosmos. It won't change anything at all. It's just one note. But it's Quinn's one note. And it matters.

His affection for the worm testified to it.

I live in a small town now, so small that the nearest Starbucks is forty-five minutes away. And even that one is at a rest stop on the highway back to somewhere. Very few of us who live here will ever be known outside of this town. We probably aren't going to attract too much attention. So it would be easy to conclude we don't matter. It would be easy to bury our passions inside us.

Which is why I can't shake the image of the silver-haired man behind the counter at the bookstore.

It's a small store. Nothing glorious. Profit margins must be miniscule. Public recognition is minimal. But every weekday at 7:00 a.m., he stands behind the counter with a smile, ready to serve the coffee of the day. And every once in a while, a kid gets to wander in and touch a book and lay a few dollars in the man's hand and walk out with a story that will transport the kid to another world. Every once in a while, an adult gets to remember what that feels like too. I think of the one note this elderly man is playing with his life, and I know, without a shadow of a doubt, that his note fits somewhere inside of a great, big, beautiful human symphony.

My affection for him testifies to it.

I can't shake the image of all the men and women in this blue-collar town who have decided their children are their passion, and they simply want to give their kids a better life than they've had. They work and they cook and they sleep (a little), and then they get up and do it again. Every day, they declare: the poverty stops here, the undereducation stops here, the dysfunction stops here. Does it matter? By some standards, I suppose not. It is an almost indistinguishable note in the great symphony of humanity. Yet you can feel the beauty of it, can't you?

Your tenderness testifies to it.

Passion isn't about proving your worth, attracting a crowd, or saving the world. It is about responding to the great ache and the mysterious affection inside of you. It's about turning your insides out until the good and beautiful thing inside of you spills out into the world.

It's about making the raw material of your life into art.

Around the time I was stifling my urge to write a book, I went to a conference for creatives. I was beginning to identify as an artist and was looking forward to learning from some kindred spirits. I needed to be inspired and had high expectations.

What I ended up inspired by, though, was their *lack* of expectations.

It turns out most artists don't do their work to achieve any particular outcome or victory, except to conquer the impulse to bury their passion deep within them. Their only goal is to turn themselves inside out, putting their passion into the world until something beautiful happens.

It's as if artists have given a megaphone to the voice of grace, so they can always hear it saying: You're not here to be great; you're here to *create*. You're not here to make a difference; you're here to make *beauty*. To make a little order out of the big chaos. To add a little abundance in a world of scarcity. You're not here to make a name for yourself; you're here to make *you* more *you* by doing what you want to do. Being an artist is simply having the audacity to add your little bit of beauty to the world.

And every single one of us can become an artist.

If your passion is gardening, for instance—if you come alive when your hands are in the dirt and the scent of watered tomato vines makes you feel like the universe has opened to you and you've been welcomed home—and if you have a ten-by-ten foot plot of land in your backyard, and if you spend your days tending to that land, cultivating it, enriching it, working it until it bears fruit (or vegetables), then in one hundred square feet of the world, your passion has a purpose that matters.

You see, the real question isn't, *Does unleashing my passion on my one hundred square feet matter?* The real question is, *If everybody on this big, broken rock tended to their one hundred square feet with their passion, would it matter? Would the world become a more beautiful and abundant place?* And if the answer to that question is yes, then garden the hell out of your one hundred square feet. Literally. Turn it into heaven.

"Let the beauty of what you love be what you do," writes the poet Rumi.

Play your one note. Beg for the dollar for the begging man. Move your worm. Find your counter to stand behind. Lift up your kids just a little higher than yourself. Write your book. Your story probably will not end up on the bestseller list. That's okay. You're not here to sell it; you're just here to *tell* it.

What is your one hundred square feet?

CHAPTER 25

Why Backward Is the New Forward

We all want progress. But progress means getting
nearer to the place where you want to be. And if you
have taken a wrong turning, then to go forward does
not get you any nearer. If you are on the wrong road,
progress means doing an about-turn and walking
back to the right road; and in that case the man who
turns back soonest is the most progressive man.

C. S. LEWIS

*H*ave you ever felt like we're all on this big rock hurtling through space and no one has any idea what the *heck* is going on?"

Remember Dante in Tennis Shoes—the young man with the business degree he didn't really want, who expressed his despair in the form of a question? Yeah, well, that wasn't the first time he had come to me for therapy. His parents had first brought him to me two years earlier, halfway through that business degree, because his drinking was a concern. During those initial sessions, I found out his dad was a businessman, and he was following closely in his father's footsteps. I also found out he cared passionately for the earth and the environment and he didn't want to *do* business; he wanted to *regulate* business to protect the planet. Back then, though, I was doing my best to make sure every kid I counseled finished college. So I weakly suggested he explore other majors, but mostly I tried to ready him for the fall semester. When the summer ended, he left for school, and I didn't hear from him again.

Then one day, I got a call.

The young man's mother told me he'd graduated, but he was languishing at home. He seemed depressed and wasn't motivated to look for a job. I found an open hour, and he came in. After he asked me his question about this big rock we're all on, he said he was miserable and told me he knew exactly why. In fact, he'd learned about it in his business major.

It's called sunk cost theory.

If you were walking to the grocery store and halfway there you heard the store was closed, would you continue to walk the rest of the way? Absolutely not, right? You'd turn around and go home or go searching for another grocery store. The distance already traveled would be a sunk cost—an investment of time you'd have to write off in order to start over and get where you want to go. When walking to the grocery store, we have no trouble accepting a sunk cost. In fact, we know it would be silly to keep walking.

But when it comes to our passions, it's a different story.

If, for instance, like Dante in Tennis Shoes, we have completed two years of college in a major we no longer enjoy, we might just continue with the degree because we've already invested so much in it. We might drink a lot to silence the voice inside urging us to turn around because it knows the "store" is closed. Then, we just might let momentum carry us down the road we no longer want to travel until, two years down that road, we wind up feeling less alive than ever before.

Now imagine going down that road for *twenty* years. And spending thousands of dollars and countless hours and all of your blood, sweat, and tears on developing a marketable skill or a career or a lifestyle you're supposed to want. Then one day, as you're hurtling right down the middle of that road, the voice of grace breaks in and the little one inside of you speaks up, and you realize that for far too long you've been living someone else's life and someone else's dream.

Where do you find brakes strong enough to break that kind of momentum?

After Dante in Tennis Shoes left my office that day, I decided part of my job as a therapist was to *become* the brakes. To discern when momentum was carrying someone down a road they didn't want to travel. To help them write off the sunk costs. To walk with them while they turn around and go back to the fork in the road, where they diverged from the path of their passion. Even if that meant helping someone drop out of college.

And, personally, I decided to press the brakes on my own life.

My dad was a therapist, and I idolized the man.

So I never considered becoming anything but a therapist, and I mimicked his professional habits. Whenever he was asked how his clinical work was going, he'd talk about how many clients he'd seen that week. So I got in the habit of viewing my work in the same way. For years, I saw ten more clients every week than the average therapist, tracked my numbers closely, and patted myself on the back for excelling at my career. But I was also burning myself out. And all the while, the voice of grace inside was urging me to write, to get out of the therapy room and into a room by myself, with just my laptop and my muse.

However, I couldn't find the brakes.

Meanwhile, my wife was doing what her mentors had done as well. Her father died when she was three and by the time she was in middle school, home was no longer a very good place to be. So she applied to boarding school and was accepted, complete with financial aid. There, she found her surrogate parents, and they were all teachers.

When she went off to college, her faculty mentor gave her something to aspire to, an academic road to race down. She continued down that road when she was admitted to graduate school. Her dissertation adviser was a rock star in academia, and my wife adored her. Professorship is a road with no speed limits, and everyone drives it with their hair on fire.

My wife was no exception.

By the age of thirty-six, she had earned her PhD in clinical psychology and been hired as junior faculty at a prestigious Christian liberal arts college, honored with a junior faculty achievement award, promoted to director of her graduate program, and awarded tenure. By the time our third child was born, she had a resume the length of a short book. And her hair was falling out. Literally.

I guess if you drive with your hair on fire long enough, it finally burns out too.

Meanwhile, nestled in her heart, hibernating for more than a decade, was her desire to actually do the therapy she'd been teaching her students about. Somewhere inside of her was the little one who knew pain and loss, and she wanted to redeem that pain by getting down on her knees, looking children in the eye, and easing a little bit of *their* pain. She wanted to go from the center of Christian culture to the margins of it, because she figured that's what Jesus would do, and she knew that's what her soul wanted to do. There was a voice inside, urging her to go back to the fork in her road and to find her true self there.

Slowly, the voice began to reveal what the fork might look like—for her and for our family. Even so, we ignored the whispers for several years. We'd get distracted and rejoin the traffic on the road we were racing, and when the voice inside each of us would whisper, we'd drown it out with obligations and commitments and schedules and habits. Sometimes when we're racing down the wrong road, we need more than the voice inside to help us put on the brakes.

We need voices on the outside too.

We need our people. Sometimes *they're* our brakes. You see, grace is persistent. It does not have a problem with rejection. It keeps whispering and waiting, loving and lingering, until we finally tell a friend about it.

About three months into the 351 days it took us to change our life, I told a friend over dinner about what we were thinking of doing. I thought he would look at me like I was crazy. Instead, he looked like he was going to cry. The joyful kind of tears. He told me it did sound crazy and it would be hard, but then he said he knew me well enough to know this: "You'll never regret it."

We told our pastor and his wife, both good friends. In the context of a marriage retreat the year before, we had shared our story with them—where we'd been and where we were at. Now we sat at our kitchen table and told them where we thought we wanted to go. She looked at us and said unequivocally, "*This* is your next chapter."

And a whole group of friends, through tears, told us how dearly we'd be missed. Then they spent six months helping us make the transition. Is there anything more loving than people who love you enough to help you leave them? Is there any love greater than the love that is willing to become a sunk cost?

Sometimes the people we belong to are the brakes we need to slow our momentum.

So we turned our lives upside down, and I learned two more lessons about sunk costs.

First, after my wife resigned from her professorship and started her new job at an upstart pediatric development center, it became clear: sunk costs are often not a total loss. It turns out the self-awareness and professional skills she developed as the director of a psychology program are also essential for running a rural health center. She never could have done the *present* thing without first having done the *previous* thing—she could not have walked the path of her true passion without first having walked the path that preceded it. In other words, the time we spend beyond the fork in the road, before we put on the brakes, is not just confusion; it's education and training. It prepares us for what lies ahead. Or rather, behind us, at the fork in the road.

Second, when I went back to the fork in *my* road, I discovered being a therapist wasn't a distraction from my passion; it was a *part* of my passion. I love my clients. They're my people too, and I'm not leaving them. My path as a psychologist isn't the wrong road; it's a parallel road—running right next to it, all along, was a second road. Back at the fork, I could finally see my passion for being a therapist *and* a writer.

Sometimes the grocery store isn't actually closed; it's just lacking something we need, and we may have to go to more than one store if we're going to find everything on our list. So I started my own practice while reducing my clinical hours by a third. Now, instead of focusing on the quantity of my therapeutic work, I focus on the quality of it, and with the extra time in my life I travel the road of my parallel passion. I go back to the fork in the road, and I write.

Please know I'm not suggesting you have to turn your world upside down. My wife and I did something radical—in a way, I still can't believe we did it—and I wouldn't recommend it for everyone. Our story is not your story. Our path is not your path. Don't ask what big changes you need to make—that's probably your shame talking, once again telling you that you must go big or go home. Instead, return to the stillness and the silence in which you rediscovered your worthiness. You might ask, *How do I get nearer to the place I want to be? Does backward need to be my new forward, for a while? Who will be my brakes?*

And what will I do, finally,
when I find my true self
back at the fork in the road?

CHAPTER 26

Courage Isn't a Character Trait
(It's a Direction)

Courage is not the absence of fear, but
rather the judgment that something
else is more important than fear.

AMBROSE HOLLINGWORTH REDMOON

The United States started bombing Afghanistan on a Sunday in October 2001.

But that's not why I remember the day.

I remember it because it was the morning my wife got onto a bus.

She's a runner. When she doesn't run, it's like a part of her has been put in time-out—it wriggles and squirms and can't wait to get out of the corner so it can start playing again. In 2001, she decided she was ready to run her first marathon. She registered for the Steamtown Marathon in Scranton, Pennsylvania, on October 7, three weeks before our wedding.

Two weeks before the race, my wife-to-be blew out her knee.

She stopped running, iced her aching joint, and tried to nurse it back to health. The day before the marathon, she was still refusing to give up on making her dream a reality, so we got in the car and headed for Scranton. We wrote our wedding vows in the hotel that night, and then, in the dark hours before dawn, I drove her to the marathon shuttle bus. The trauma of 9/11 still hung in the air—like bagpipes in the distance that won't stop playing—and race officials wanted to reduce spectators near the main event by shuttling runners to the starting line.

The image of her is seared in my mind: her stepping out of the warm car into the biting autumn air, on a knee she wasn't sure she could trust, to run a race most of us can't imagine running, all by herself, not knowing a soul. The overhead lights of the bus were on, so I could see her mounting the steps and shuffling through the crowded aisle to find a seat by herself near the back.

Later in the day, as bombing in Afghanistan commenced, thousands of men and women and children would be plunged into a conflict requiring an epic kind of bravery. But watching her through the window, I knew I was witnessing another kind of bravery—the everyday kind of bravery it takes to do what we want to do in the world. It may not win a Purple Heart, but it won *my* heart.

Because it was the true definition of *courage*.

The word *courage* is derived from the Latin root *cor*, which means "heart." Unfortunately, we've played fast and loose with the original meaning of the word *heart*. The dictionary defines *courage* as "the quality of mind or spirit that enables a person to face difficulty, danger, pain, etc., without fear." We have taken "heart" and turned it into a Mel Gibson movie about a mythical Scottish warrior. We have made courage into something you do on a battlefield, without flinching. A more faithful translation of the Latin root *cor* still includes "heart," but it understands "heart" to mean *center*, as in "the heart of the matter."

Cor means *core.*

To have courage is simply to be who you are at your core and to follow your passion. It's not a character trait; it's a *direction.* People aren't born with courage; people are born with passions—things we're here to do. Courage is simply the decision to move toward them. So, true courage, to the observer, might look quite mundane, because it's ordinary people doing the ordinary things they are here to do.

Just one teeny, tiny step at a time.

Adolescence is a social bloodbath—hormones and shame are multiplying, and little egos are hitting puberty too, growing quickly and learning how to defend and attack at a precipitous rate. Entire personas are built and laid to waste between class periods. Any moment can become a hinge—a wrinkle in time that sends your life spinning in one direction or another. Sometimes we step toward who we are becoming. Sometimes we don't. Courage can start here, because courage is simply the good habit of stepping in the direction we want to go, regardless of the fear, uncertainty, or risk that stands in the way.

I have a friend who lives down the street in our new neighborhood. He's a pediatrician and a leader in the local medical community. In eighth grade, he got in the habit of stepping in the right direction while attending an American international school, where a bunch of older, bigger boys tried to bully him. On the first day of school, a group of upper classmen cornered him in the lunchroom and ordered him to get them something to drink. He asked how many were in their group. They said eleven. So, trembling a little on the inside, he looked the ringleader directly in the eye and said, "Good, that

means you've got twenty-two hands; I'm sure you can manage it."
And then he stepped toward them and *through* them, as the group
parted for him.

They never picked on him again.

What do my wife and my friend have in common? Do they have
hardier hearts, sturdier souls, or better character than the rest of
us? No. It's not about their hearts at all. It's about their feet. They're
determined to move in the direction of who they are. Courage is that
simple. It doesn't mean you're more confident or certain or fearless
or tough or strong or successful or valiant or heroic. It means you're
committed. To a direction.

In the third act of life, you step in the direction of the passion
at your core.

We live in a leap-before-you-look culture.

When you read about finding your passion and pursuing your
dreams, the advice is often, "Just leap!" As if your passion is something you do in a moment, a one-and-done event in which you face
your fear, make a single decision, and change your life for good. But
the truth is, moving toward your passion is a lot less like jumping
into the deep end of a pool and a lot more like wading into the ocean.
It happens gradually, one step at a time. You often can't see the ocean
floor. You don't know when it's going to drop away and the water is
going to get deeper. You don't know what's in there waiting to take
a nip at your toes or sting your skin.

But you just keep moving forward.

You sign up for the photography class. Choose a domain name.
Sit down in front of the blank page. Or easel. Go to your first yoga
certification training. Schedule coffee with someone who is already

doing what you want to do. Create an Etsy shop. Buy a book about parenting. Or write one. Charter a landscaping business during the day while working as a chef at night. Start coaching Little League. Turn in an application. You stare into the dark dawn before the race, or into the eyes of the ringleader, and then you step *toward* them.

Because you need to walk through the scary stuff to get to the good stuff.

In October 2011—exactly a decade after my wife completed the Steamtown marathon—I started practicing courage by marching to the beat of my own soul. I dipped my toe into the ocean by setting up a few social media accounts, purchasing a URL, starting a blog, writing my first post, and publishing it. When nobody read it, I took another step anyway, and I published another one. No one read that one either. But now my passion couldn't be shoved back into the bedside table. So I took a few more steps.

Seven weeks later, I wrote one a bunch of people read.

Step.

So I started an e-mail list.

Step.

I wrote a short e-book and gave it away free to anyone who subscribed to the blog.

Step.

Every week, no matter how scary it was, I put my words out there.

Step.

Then a letter to my daughter went viral. I was in up to my waist.

Step.

A second letter went viral and the *TODAY* show called. In way over my head.

Step.

I got connected with a literary agent.

Step.

An editor took a chance on my book.

Step.

Now I'm writing chapter twenty-six of that book.

It's how our passions unfold. One step at a time. Like wading into the ocean. Of course, like wading into the ocean, the big waves will come—the big fear will arise or your knee will give way or the bullies won't go away—but you will begin to trust something very counterintuitive about your fear. Like standing in the ocean with a big wave coming at you, you don't stand still and let it crash down on you, turning you upside down. And you certainly don't run away from it, turning your back on it and letting it slam you from behind into the rocky ocean floor. No, you move toward your fear and dive into it before it breaks. Then you learn you can slice through it cleanly and come back up for air. You learn that moving toward the thing you love is the only way worth going. Even if fear stands between it and you.

That's what courage is.

But I'm not telling you something you don't already know. Indeed, I'm not even telling you something you haven't already *done*. After all, there is a little one in you who walked into that first day of kindergarten—just a big backpack sitting on top of two little legs—stepping into and through your fear.

You've taken steps like this all your life, haven't you?

When you went to the birthday party, not knowing anyone but the birthday boy. When you got on the bus for the first day of middle school. When you interviewed for that first job. Reported for your first day of work. Sent off those college applications. Said yes to a marriage. Or ended one. Felt the first contraction. Pressed send on the painful e-mail. Heard the diagnosis. Survived the surgery. Called the therapist. Dropped a kid off at college. In fact, you took a step this morning, when you woke up and got up and moved into the dark dawn and big bullies of an ordinary day.

You can do this. You *have* done this.

Now, though, you have a chance to do it for a new reason. For your *passion*.

— CHAPTER 27 —

Why There Was No Crowd at the Foot of the Cross

"Eli, Eli, lema sabachthani?"

MATTHEW 27:46

Quinn holds out his hand to show me his thumbnail.

Or lack thereof.

The end of it has been ripped clean off. He says he hit it on the jungle gym while playing tag at recess. A day earlier, his nose had been bloodied when his face lost a battle with a kid's head on the same playground. And a week earlier he had told me the top of his head was bruised after he flew headlong into one of the slides on the playground. I look at him incredulously and say, "Dude, you're taking a beating on the playground." He frowns, shakes his head, and says, "Yeah, I guess it's not meant for me."

I guess it's not meant for me.

This is what we do. When we start to take some hits on the playground of life, we assume we're on the wrong playground or we simply shouldn't be playing at all. We human beings tend to treat our circumstances like divining rods, using good fortune and hardship to determine if we're on the right path and in good favor with the powers—or the Power—that be. When things are breaking bad,

203

we interpret our misfortune and disappointment as a cosmic course correction. When things are going well, we believe our choices have received a divine stamp of approval. Either way, it's comforting to feel like we have a heavenly tour guide.

Of course, sometimes we're *not* meant to do the thing we're trying to do. For example, when I was cut from the middle school choral ensemble, I decided singing wasn't for me. Twenty years later, when my kids began asking me to either sing their lullabies "like Momma does" or not to sing them at all, because it was hurting their ears, I realized the wisdom of my middle school decision.

And it's equally true that when we're courageously stepping through our fears and into our passions, the universe often seems to open up for us. Tumblers fall into place, doors swing wide, and warm winds fill our sails day after smooth-sailing day. We seem to have fallen into lockstep with a purpose or a plan more ancient than time itself.

Yet, whenever we pursue a passion that is an authentic expression of our true self, we will also experience misfortune, disappointment, hardship, and pain. Because when we're pursuing our passions, our souls are out there, exposed, vulnerable. There's no way to practice a passion without leaving ourselves wide open for wounding. Like Quinn on the playground, we will get bruised, bloody, and beat up. So, if you're going to step into your passion, it's probably a good idea to take a big box of Band-Aids into it with you.

Instead, we tend to take our divining rods into it.

For instance, when I was nearing the end of graduate school, I was in a church small group full of other young and ambitious students, and as the time approached for graduation, the divining rods came out: "I can't find an apartment in Philly; God must not want me there." Or "I didn't get the internship; maybe God doesn't want me to be a chemist." Of course, it all boiled down to this: *I'm*

getting banged up on this here playground, so I guess it's not meant for me.
This subtle belief is a big reason so many passions aren't lived out.

And it's why there was no crowd at the foot of the cross.

In the story central to my faith, Jesus begins the final week of his life
with a triumphal entry into the holy city of Jerusalem. The crowds
turn out en masse. He looks like a man who is doing all the right
things and making all the right moves. He has no bruises on his
head, no bloody nose, no broken thumbnail. To the crowd, it looks
like God is on his side, and he looks like the savior they've been
waiting for—the one who will lead the revolution to free Israel from
the grip of the Roman Empire. It looks like he's found his messianic
purpose.

So they lay palm leaves at his feet and cheer wildly. Yet before
they have a chance to catch their breath, his good fortune goes bad.
Instead of being celebrated by the Jewish authorities, he comes
into conflict with them. A major bruise to the head. Then one of
his disciples betrays him, and he's arrested. A bloody nose on the
messianic playground. Then he's beaten and brutalized and hung
upon a cross—the ultimate torture and shame in his culture. It
makes a bloody thumbnail look like, well, child's play.

In the span of a week, he's gone from having an obvious stamp
of divine approval to being banged up and beaten, a sign to the
crowds of divine rejection. You see, pursuing our passions makes no
sense to a world that still believes the path of passion is paved only
with good fortune and signs of divine blessing. It makes no sense
to people who still believe hardship is a consequence for making the
wrong decision or choosing the wrong path. So the crowds look at
Jesus and decide it wasn't meant to be.

And they go away.

Even Jesus, as he hangs on the cross, in a moment of excruciating solidarity with all our suffering humanity, experiences his pain as abandonment when he looks up and cries out, *"Eli, Eli, lema sabachthani?"* My God, my God, why have you forsaken me?

The third act of a story contains the climactic moment of the story. It is the moment on which the protagonist's story hinges—will the character we have come to love finally succumb to the conflict, or resolve it? In the third act of life, it's the moment when our dedication to the passions we're living is tested, and we have a choice: we can *go* back, or we can *call* back, "I'm all in. This is what I'm here to do, and I'll do it until I can't do it anymore."

In these pages, I've described passion as "an extravagant fondness." However, the word *passion* was originally derived from a Latin root meaning "to suffer." What if both are true at the same time? What if a passion is something we are so extravagantly fond of doing—so central to who we are—that we would also choose to suffer for it, if necessary? The climactic moment in the third act of life is the moment you realize you've truly found your purpose, because you've found a passion you refuse to give up on even if the crowd gives up on you.

I used to assume resurrection was the climactic moment of the Jesus story. Now, though, I think the climax of his story was the moment of his greatest despair. I imagine Jesus looking up and crying out to God, who seems to have abandoned him, and then I imagine him looking down and locking eyes with the only three people who remained at the foot of the cross—his mother, a friend, and a follower. I imagine him looking into the eyes of the people he belonged to—the people who still believed in him even when things looked bleakest—and finding there the strength to carry on. In our climactic moment, our people go beyond simply pointing us toward our passion—they become *compassion*, a word meaning, literally, "to suffer with." The people we belong to are the ones who choose to remain with us as we choose to suffer for the thing we're here to do.

The story of Jesus' cross is an extraordinary one—some have called it the greatest story ever told. The crosses we choose to suffer tend to be much more ordinary.

I decided a while back that, among other things, I'm on this planet to write a book. I decided it was my passion, and I decided to suffer for it, if necessary. In that sense, I suppose, it is a cross I have chosen to carry. And it's tempting to think the publication of it will be the climactic moment in this particular third act of my life. But when I think about Jesus hanging on the cross, crying out in despair and then looking down into the eyes of the three who remained—his mother, Mary Magdalene, and John—I realize my climactic moment happened months ago.

After writing and trashing more than two hundred thousand words over the course of almost two years, I found thirteen thousand words that worked for a book proposal. When my agent first approached several publishing houses and they saw the volume of my blog traffic, many were eager to see the proposal.

But then we sent the actual proposal, and the many quickly dispersed.

It was "too spiritual" for some and "not Christian enough" for others. Some wanted only a book of letters to my kids, while others wanted a book about marriage. Most didn't think I had the credentials to write about passion and purpose. Nobody thought they could bank on it. They wanted me to write a completely different book.

In that moment, I wanted to quit—bruised head, bleeding nose, broken thumbnail—because I thought this author playground wasn't meant for me. I thought maybe I was supposed to be doing something else, and I wanted that something else to feel less like death and more like resurrection. But then, at the foot of the cross-passion I had chosen, my faithful agent said she wouldn't let me write anything else, because she believed in it too much. I looked into the eyes of my wife, and she said the same thing. And this whole lovely cloud of witnesses around the world, who read my blog every week, kept letting me know they weren't going anywhere. Suddenly, the presence of those who remained mattered more than the opinion of the dwindling crowd.

I got back on the playground and decided to keep playing. To keep writing.

I hope you will too. I hope you'll pick up your cross-passion and carry it. Not necessarily because it will lead to resurrection, but because the sacrifice alone is worth it. After all, sacrifice isn't the way *to* heaven; sacrifice is the way *of* heaven. It's where your commitment to the thing you're here to do will be tested and refined, where your circles of belonging will be proven steadfast, and where you'll learn all over again: you are worthy, whether you wind up leading a revolution, or simply returning to the playground, Band-Aids and all, for a little more play.

Because it *is* meant for you.

CHAPTER 28

The Redemptive Relationship Between Passion, Pain, and Purpose

Listen to your life. See it for the fathomless
mystery it is. In the boredom and pain of it, no
less than in the excitement and gladness: touch,
taste, smell your way to the holy and hidden heart
of it, because in the last analysis all moments
are key moments, and life itself is grace.

FREDERICK BUECHNER

*A*s the third act of this book draws to a close, I want to speak now specifically to those among us who might—even after coming this far along the path of worthiness, belonging, and purpose—still feel . . . **purposeless.** I want you to know, there is nothing wrong with you. It is not at all unusual to practice a passion, to suffer for it, to be buoyed by the compassion of your people, and to still feel as if some essential element of your story is missing. This is because our passion—while exhilarating and energizing—can still feel meaningless in and of itself. Sometimes our passion can feel like a Tasmanian devil, spinning madly in endless directions. Sometimes

passion needs something to contain it, to focus it, and to turn it in
a direction that is good, holy, and meaningful. And sometimes that
something is our pain.

Or more specifically, the *redemption* of it.

I just deleted six hours' worth of writing.

Why? Because an essential element of a meaningful story might
be a wound redeemed, but how do I write about redeeming pain
without sounding trite, without inadvertently glorifying agony,
without my words ringing hollow, being dismissive, or sounding cold
and cruel? How do I write about the value of pain without leaving
everyone who's *in* pain—in other words, most of us—feeling a little
devalued? How do I suggest to those who have survived horrors—
incest, rape, beatings, neglect, ridicule, starvation, genocide, natural
and manmade disasters, depression, loneliness, anxiety, panic—that
pain may not *have* a purpose, but it might be the one thing that can
give us a purpose, through its redemption? After six hours of trying,
it finally occurred to me: I can't.

Delete.

But what I can do is acknowledge that pain never feels promising; it usually feels, well, painful. Pain can wreck a day and a year
and a life and it can make us question the presence of a Love big
enough to make all things well. So, yeah. Pain. I have no interest
in sugar-coating it.

But I am interested in *redeeming* it.

We have a lot of important relationships in life, but among the most important is our relationship to pain. And we have all sorts of unhealthy ways of relating to it: we resist it, avoid it, ignore it, numb it, transfer it, and allow it to plunge us into apathy, despair, and fatalism. Our relationship to pain—our *response* to it—is usually determined by how we define pain. For our purpose (see what I did there?), I want to suggest a definition of pain that has begun to transform my relationship to it: pain is mess—misfortune and disorder, mistakes and chaos—that we feel really, really intensely.

This definition helps me because it means I can start to relearn my response to really big pain by understanding how I relate to even the smallest messes. And if I think of it that way, then being a father is teaching me an awful lot about pain by confronting me with just how dysfunctional my relationship to relatively miniscule messes has been. What I mean is, before kids, I could mostly order my world the way I wanted to. I could put everything in its proper place, prevent most mistakes, and keep the chaos mostly at bay. But kids. Sheesh.

They multiply mess like wet gremlins.

They shoot poop out of their diapers onto your lap, spray urine into their own faces when you open the diaper, vomit on everything, fall down and bleed on your new shorts, spill something as soon as the meal begins, and color on the walls. They get disgusting diseases with disgusting names like conjunctivitis. And on the way from the hotel to the *TODAY* show, the little one in the white tights spills red smoothie all over her legs and your pants. Then, backstage, the older two spill coffee on themselves and orange juice on the floor.

When you have kids, the other guests at NBC give you a *lot* of space.

So, as a father, I've had two options. The first is to announce we are simply not a mess kind of family and to ban any additional messes. Of course, I know that's a bad idea. My kids would feel ashamed of their natural mess-making talents. They'd feel controlled by—and rebellious toward—all my attempts to enforce the ban. Plus, it would be futile, because the messes aren't going away. So instead I've gone with option number two, a new policy: it's okay to make messes, as long as you clean them up.

It turns out one of the great, surprising pleasures of parenting is watching my kids clean up their disasters. And it's downright *breathtaking* to watch one of their siblings voluntarily join them in cleaning up the mess they've made. These days, when a mess happens, I yearn for the moment when one of my kids sees a sibling laboring to clean up a mess, stops, takes a knee, gets right down into the chaos with them, and says, "I'll clean it up with you."

I'll redeem it with you.

The whole thing has made me less resistant to little messes and to big pain and, even, to God. Now, I figure God is like a parent, and we're all like God's kids, and I'm guessing God has known from the beginning what I've had to learn as I go: a father can't meddle to prevent every mess or his kids will hate him, and it wouldn't work anyway because the kids are mess-making machines, so mess is going to happen one way or another. Yeah, I think God's been doing for eternity what I've barely begun to do: just watching and waiting and anticipating the joy of his children coming together to clean up the mess and redeem the pain.

Our relationship to pain doesn't change all at once, though. The other day, our family watched the movie *McFarland, USA*—a true story about a bunch of impoverished, blue-collar, Latino boys who (spoiler alert!) beat the odds and won the California state high school cross-country championship. *Nine* times. The boys in McFarland are great cross-country runners because they know pain—they spend long, grueling days in the fields, bent over in the blistering sun, picking crops. As the film progresses, one clear theme emerges: if you can welcome your pain, you can climb any hill.

My kids loved the movie.

The next day, we went on our first family bike ride in our new town. To get out of our neighborhood, you have to descend a great slope that had Caitlin squealing with delight behind me on our tandem bike. To get back into the neighborhood, you have to ascend that same slope, and it had Quinn screaming with agony, "I can't do it, Daddy!" as his little legs pushed against the pedals.

So I said to him, "Buddy, remember McFarland. You can choose to walk away from the pain and walk the rest of the way up this hill. If you do, I'll understand completely, and I'll walk with you. Or you can welcome the pain along for the ride and choose to keep going upward anyway. If you do, we'll keep pedaling with you." And, for a day at least, he changed his relationship to pain. He embraced it, and he let it ride tandem with him up a really big hill. Neither stopped until they got to the top.

Our relationship to pain changes slowly, one redemptive embrace at a time.

This is true of physical pain *and* emotional pain.

At the age of 10, sage and comedian Stephen Colbert experienced enough tragedy for a lifetime, when his father and two of his brothers were killed in a plane crash. His other siblings were already grown and gone, leaving him alone with his mother. According to Colbert, he was saved from his grief by a number of blessings including his mother's love, his faith, and his love for books.

But mostly he was saved by improvisational comedy.

Before his first night on a professional stage, Second City

director Jeff Michalski told him, "You have to learn to love the bomb." The key to improv—the key to getting up on stage without a script, the key to making art in the midst of the mess—is learning to love the mess. You have to embrace the fear of screwing up and the pain of failure. Colbert says, "The discomfort and the wishing that it would end that comes around you. I would do things like that and just breathe it in. Nope, can't kill me. This thing can't kill me."

Through improv, Colbert learned how to accept suffering.

"Which," he adds, "does not mean being defeated by suffering. Acceptance is not defeat. Acceptance is just awareness. 'You gotta learn to love the bomb.' Boy, did I have a bomb when I was 10. That was quite an explosion. And I learned to love it . . . That might be why you don't see me as someone angry and working out my demons onstage. It's that I love the thing that I most wish had not happened."

Colbert not only embraced his pain; he learned to love it.

Sometimes, redeeming our pain is about coming to value it so much, we let it *lead* us.

As my son was riding up the hill on his little mountain bike, my daughter and I followed on our tandem bike. She pedaled madly in the rear and I rode up front, steering us in the right direction. For some of us, I think purpose has to be like a tandem bike: passion pedals joyfully and furiously from the back seat, and pain sits up front, steering our passion *upward*. In other words, pain doesn't have to be a roadblock to a purposeful life; sometimes it can actually be a road sign.

It points our passion in a holy direction.

What I'm about to say is the closest I'll ever get to declaring something a rule: where our most vibrant passion meets our most visceral pain, we discover a sense of purpose. It happens so consistently it's almost a natural law of the universe, like gravity: our passion becomes our purpose when it redeems our pain. When you do what the little one in you loves to do, in the service of redeeming that little one's pain, it feels like you're playing your one note and playing it beautifully. To be clear, I'm not saying redeeming your pain with your passion is the *only* way to redeem your pain. But I am suggesting it can be one of the most joyful, rewarding, and meaningful ways to do so.

And there's more. Once you've begun to redeem your pain with your passion, you will almost inevitably feel drawn to redeem that same kind of wound in the world as well. Perhaps that is what theologian and author Frederick Buechner meant when he wrote, "The place God calls you to is the place where your deep gladness and the world's deep hunger meet."

For instance, if you have a passion for psychology and counseling, you probably won't practice just any kind of therapy; you'll practice the kind that will redeem the wound inside of you—if you were an anxious kid, you'll focus on healing anxiety in others. Or if you grew up with leukemia and have a passion for nursing and want to find the deepest meaning and sense of purpose in it, you probably won't work in the ER; you'll work in the pediatric oncology unit. When my wife ran that marathon in Scranton on her bum knee, she wasn't just pursuing her passion, she was also redeeming her pain with it. The girl who lost her father when she was three was running to raise money for foster children.

Purpose is what inevitably happens when your passion heals something that has been wounded, repairs something that has been broken, resurrects something that has died, or redeems something that has gone awry. If you discover this kind of purpose, one day you might find yourself climbing the hill of your life, looking back at the road you've traveled, remembering the pain you've redeemed, and realizing you've come to love the thing you most wish had not happened.

"That is what mortals misunderstand," writes C. S. Lewis. "They say of some temporal suffering, 'No future bliss can make up for it,' not knowing that Heaven, once attained, will work backwards and turn even that agony into a glory."

I don't know what your pain is, but I do know you're human, so I know you have some. I know there is a little one inside of you with wounds waiting for healing. I know there is a voice of grace whispering as well, waiting to point you toward the mess in your story that is most in need of cleaning up. And I know when you bring your passion to bear upon the redemption of that pain, a sense of purpose is a foregone conclusion.

And that's not such a bad way to end a third act.

CHAPTER 29

A Peace That Surpasses All Understanding

You do not have to be good.
You do not have to walk on your knees
for a hundred miles through the desert, repenting.
You only have to let the soft animal of your body
    love what it loves.
Tell me about your despair, yours, and I will tell you mine.
Meanwhile the world goes on.
Meanwhile the sun and the clear pebbles of the rain
are moving across the landscapes,
over the prairies and the deep trees,
the mountains and the rivers.
Meanwhile the wild geese, high in the clean blue air,
are heading home again.
Whoever you are, no matter how lonely,
the world offers itself to your imagination,
calls to you like the wild geese, harsh and exciting—
over and over announcing your place
in the family of things.

MARY OLIVER, "WILD GEESE"

This morning, as I stood at my kitchen sink, a veil was lifted.

We moved into our new home almost four months ago, in the throes of a hot, wet summer that had transformed central Illinois into a tropical backwater. The forests were like jungles and the only thing thicker than the vegetation was the mosquitoes. But, like all seasons, it eventually passed, replaced by cooler days and dwindling light.

Our kitchen window looks out on the road that runs in front of our house, and across the road is a forest of trees. When we moved in, those trees were thick with leaves and underbrush. We were surrounded by green as far as the eye could see, and it looked like we were alone. Cut off from the rest of the world. Divided. Apart. Yet as the autumn winds have arisen and the temperatures have fallen, so have the leaves. This morning as I cleaned the breakfast dishes, I looked up and looked out, and was startled by what I saw.

Through the trees, I saw houses.

Lots of them. With lights on in the dark, dawning hour. People moving to and fro. Doing their own dishes. Getting their own kids ready for school. Behind curtains, getting dressed for work. A whole community of people preparing to do another day together. Each household one part of a greater whole.

As the warm water washed over my hands, a warm awareness washed over *me*.

We were never alone. We were never apart. Never divided. We were always close, always connected by the road that runs by our house and curves around to those homes on the other side of the trees. I just couldn't see it. Because I couldn't see through the leaves.

In the end, this is what our stories do for us when we live them in the order they are meant to be lived. They gradually usher us into a new season in which our illusion of separateness falls away, like fading leaves in autumn. One by one, the dying remnants of our shame drop to the ground. The leaves of ego gradually wither and release. Our fear of meaninglessness is pulled free in a gentle breeze of passion and purpose. And then we can finally see with clarity that this journey we're on isn't just about being healed.

It is ultimately about being *wholed*.

The Hebrew word for peace is *shalom*. Its literal translation is "completeness" or "wholeness." Shalom is not the absence of conflict; it is the absence of division. To experience shalom in our lives is to have no division within our being, within our loving, or within our living. The three acts of our story, it turns out, are a gradual progression toward unity within our self, our relationships, and what we choose to do with our days. A progression toward wholeness, which is to say, *peace*.

In the first act of life, we begin to overcome the disunity at the center of our *self*, which was wrought by our shame. We embrace the confused and lost little one in us, we return to our worthy and good-enough soul, and we come back into union with the divine spark underneath our underneath. We coalesce around our true self.

The healing is a wholing.

In the second act of life, we begin to overcome the disunity at the center of our relationships. The division between our false self and our true self is bridged. The two parts of our self find a place of acceptance and belonging with each other and, as our soul and our ego find a way to coexist as one, our relationships and marriages and communities are made one as well.

The healing is a wholing.

In the third act of life, we begin to mend the division between what we want to do and what we actually do. The passion that has been hibernating in our souls is awakened and finds expression in the activity of our daily lives. Who we *are* on the inside and what we *do* on the outside become one.

The healing is a wholing.

Finally, as the curtain falls on the third act of life, it begins to dawn on us that this voice of grace we've been hearing has been, all along, whispering in the language of *wholeness*. And what was once a foreign language to us has, increasingly, over the course of three acts, become our native tongue. Now, if we listen closely, we can hear that the story of our personal wholeness is not the only story being told.

A bigger story is being told, about the wholeness of *everyone*.

As I stood at the sink watching the lights through the autumn trees, Aidan was skittering around the kitchen in a panic. The night before, he'd spent his after-school hours lighting up the world with his passions—three hours of rehearsal for his upcoming musical, an hour's worth of learning called homework, and thirty minutes of guitar practice. He simply hadn't had the time to make his lunch for the next day. So, with only minutes before he needed to catch his ride to school, he was panicking, because organization and planning are not his strengths. He can remember every line in *The Little Mermaid*, but under pressure, he can't remember how to make a peanut butter and jelly sandwich. So instead of making a sandwich, he decided to make *wholeness*.

He turned to Quinn, who *does* have a passion for organization and planning and speed and efficiency. Quinn gets home from school and makes his lunch for the next day before his siblings have shed their coats. He doesn't do it because he *has* to; he does it because he *loves* to. It's the beauty in him spread between two pieces of bread. And his big brother knows it.

So Aidan looked at his younger brother and said, "Quinn, I'll nominate you for an act of kindness if you help me put my lunch together." Quinn was immediately on his feet with a smile on his face. Not only because an act of kindness will earn him privileges within our family system, but also because his passion had been recognized and called upon. Because his older brother had been like the wild geese calling, harsh and exciting, reminding him of his valuable place in our family of things.

It was peace, in the best sense of the word, because it was shalom—people coming together, mingling their passions, functioning as one, as a whole. It's the final wholeness—the big wholiness. We're all in this together, or as the apostle Paul might say, we're all invaluable parts of a single body. It is a shalom that surpasses all understanding.

The big story is about the wholeness of everyone. And *everything.*

A week later, the leaves are falling and thinning as I enter the forest path.

Then I hear it.

The forest I'm in extends for miles in every direction; it's a county-wide canopy of drying autumn leaves, and I can hear the wind approaching me on the treetops. It's like a great rushing whisper, like a wave of something omnipotent but invisible. It comes to me like grace.

And it *is* grace.

Because grace is always getting bigger. Whereas we once experienced grace as the still, small voice of God inside of us, it eventually and inevitably expands. From inside of you to outside of you. From small to vast. From one place to every place. From whisper to wind. And finally, like the wind, it comes at you from all angles.

The voice I once heard only on the inside, I now hear on the wind: *You're not here to be happy, Kelly, or to be productive or wealthy or victorious or celebrated; you're here to be* whole. *To be wholly* you. *And you're here to know you are part of a greater whole—part of a greater oneness, without divisions. You're here for shalom. You're here to be at peace.*

The wind subsides and the subtle sounds of the wood return. And I hear grace in all of them. The sandpaper rasp of browning cornstalks in the fields. The buzz of bees on a dying bud. A single bird, warbling in the distance. The tap-knocking of a languid woodpecker. The constant background hum of crickets who have forgotten it's daytime. The sound of something unseen, but big and powerful, crashing through underbrush nearby.

From a distance, a man approaches me, led by a large Labrador. The dog pants softly and the man breathes heavily. Our eyes meet. We nod and smile. His eyes soften—years of crinkles at the corners come alive. I suspect mine do too. But in that moment, I know, we have more in common than our aging skin. We have something *underneath* our skin. We have a spark of God embedded in the core of us. We come from the same place, rays emanating from the same Light. We are fragments of a breathtaking whole. Separated by our skin, but joined by our souls. Siblings of Something bigger and better than the best parent we can imagine. Birthed by Love, separated at birth, and now reunited. For a moment.

Two stray geese honk overhead, announcing our place in the family of things.

The man and his dog pass by. I smell the sweet-rot of a world winding down for another winter. It mingles with the ashy scent of smoke coming on the wind from some unknown place, and the sharp scent of brittle air coming down from the north. The cloud-covered sky is platinum, like precious metal. The voice of grace is in all of it. Every sight and sound and smell. Grace comes from every direction and every angle, and is the bridge between all things. Grace is the common denominator making all things one, the shalom making all things whole.

Grace is a mystery that keeps getting bigger with every act of the story. But that's the way the best stories work: they don't answer all our questions; they leave us asking better ones. Listen to the voice of grace, know you are loveable, and be whole. Shed your shame. Let go of your lonely. Turn your insides out and live passionately into your purpose now. And, by grace, find your place in the great, big, beautiful family of things.

It's why you're here.

A Last Letter to My Little Ones
(in Case I'm Not Around for the Important Moments)

Dear Little Ones,

I wrote this book for you because I could die any day.

Don't worry. I'm not sick. I'm just human, which is to say fragile and fleeting and unable to know when it's all going to end. Your momma thinks I'm silly for thinking about that all the time. And maybe I am. But I just can't seem to help it. So I wrote every word of this book with you in mind.

The whole time, I was thinking of what I may not be around for:

Aidan, I thought of you in middle school, with your first crush and your first dance coming up. I thought about you maybe asking her to go and her maybe saying no. I thought about all the things the rejection might cause you to conclude about who you are, who you are not, and how worthy you may or may not be to belong. I thought about not being there to hug you when that happens.

And it made me ache.

Quinn, I thought about your passion for soccer and how, whenever you put on your shin guards, you put on a smile. I thought about how much you love to play goalie and how much you pride yourself on shutting out the other team. I thought of how it's going to feel when the boys get bigger and faster and stronger and you can't block every ball anymore. I thought about the way a passion can get smothered when it gets all tangled up with performance. I thought about the smile finally dropping from your face. I thought about not being there to lift up your chin when that happens.

And it made me ache.

Caitlin, I thought about the joy you bring to everything—how you can turn any fake laugh into a real laugh, and how you can turn any real laugh into a memory. But I thought, too, about those moments when I speak a little too harshly to you, or come down a little too hard on you. I thought about the way your chin quivers and your eyes irrigate. And I thought, if I can accidentally do that to your heart with a *tone*, what will the world do to your heart with *intent?* I thought about not being there to wipe away your tears.

And it made me ache.

For each of you, I thought about all the things I may not be around to speak into—all the nights before the big tests and the moments before the big games and the graduations and college applications and the first day of your first big job. Or the day you scrap it all to choose art over business. I thought about the day you'll ask someone to marry you or get asked by someone to marry them or decide marriage isn't for you. I thought about the day your first child is born, adopted, or miscarried, or the day you decide parenthood isn't for you. I thought about not being there for you to lean on.

And it made me ache.

So just in case fortune doesn't smile upon me, I wrote a book for you. I wanted you to know everything I know about how the road to peace goes through worthiness, belonging, and purpose. But the truth is, something a little disconcerting happened in the middle of it: what I know *changed* while I wrote.

For instance, I set out to write a book about banishing shame; instead, the book started writing *me*.

Now I know, we don't banish our shame. We redeem it, slowly, over the course of a lifetime. It never goes away completely. It's always waiting for us around the next bend in the road. When I began, I thought we *evict* shame from our lives; now I know we can *expect* shame in our lives. And when it turns up once more, we welcome it as an opportunity to listen once again for the voice of grace.

I set out to write a book about conquering the ego; instead, the book started writing *me*.

Now I know we don't conquer our ego. We *talk* with it and try to speak some sense into it. If we're gentle and persistent, then gradually, over time, we get through to it and it goes into hibernation for a season. And what a beautiful season it is! A season of vulnerability and connection and belonging and unloneliness. Of course, the season always ends—the ego always awakens from its slumber—and then we begin the conversation all over again.

I set out to write a book about world-changing purpose: instead, the book started writing *me*.

Now I know there are no world changers. We're not here to be superheroes. We're here simply to do our thing. To let our passion out, to commit to it and suffer for it if necessary, to redeem some bit of our pain with it, and to find joy in that. So much joy that other people take notice and want to have a little of what we have. We're here to quietly ignite an epidemic of that kind of purpose-fullness. Little Ones, the world doesn't need you to change it; it needs you to *love* it, by doing what you're here to do.

I started this book when I was thirty-six. Now I'm thirty-nine. Almost everything I thought I knew changed in three years. How much more will change in the next three? What would I have written if I'd waited until I was fifty-nine to tell you? I can't know. And I couldn't wait. Because there may not be a fifty-nine for me. Yet, it's a good reminder we're all learning as we go. Little Ones, give yourselves the grace to think you know what you know, to realize you don't, and then to learn it all over again.

And the last thing I want you to know is this: not *everything* changed for me while I wrote. I never stopped believing in the importance of living a good story.

Little Ones, live the kind of story you'd want to read. The kind of story where you fall in love with every character, find the goodness in all of them, and desperately desire for the brokenness in everybody to be redeemed. *Choose for yourself what you'd choose for the most beloved characters in your favorite stories.*

And then, regardless of how it all turns out, I trust I'll see you on the other side, when we exchange this flesh-and-blood mystery for the mystery that comes after. Because, I believe, there's a story being told there too.

Yours forever,

Dad

Seasons, Sequels, and Souls

And the end of all our exploring
Will be to arrive where we started
And to know the place for the first time.

T. S. ELIOT

We're all traveling in circles.

I live in a part of the world where the earth won't let you ignore that fact. We have seasons. I think of autumn as the beginning—the point we're always returning to—probably because I usually think of dying as a new beginning rather than an end. So in my part of the world, autumn invites us into winding down, into stillness. Winter invites us to gather together with our people around a warm hearth, to draw closer, to rest, and to be restored. Then spring invites us into resurrection, into action and vibrancy and life. And finally, summer invites us all to come together, to congregate and celebrate outdoors, to enjoy the bounty emerging from our circular journey.

Then, of course, we find ourselves in the dying season again.

I'm grateful for the seasons. I'm glad to be reminded everything cycles, everything comes and goes and comes again. Without the seasons, I might every year hurtle millions of miles through space, only to return to the same place and never realize it. The seasons go in a circle, and the whole planet orbits in a circle and rotates in a circle and *is* a circle of sorts. Our lives go in circles too—we come from the darkness of the womb and return to the darkness of the grave—from ashes to ashes and dust to dust. Every day and year and life, it seems, comes back around to where it began.

Does this sound like fatalism? Does it sound like I'm saying we never really get anywhere? Because that's not what I mean. What I mean is, the kind of progress we've been talking about in these pages follows the same pattern as the rest of life and the universe: it happens in circles. As I mentioned earlier, my psychiatrist friend pointed out that spiritual growth is like climbing a mountain. It's not linear and you can't race straight up the side of it. You have to circle the mountain gradually.

In our lives, we may circle the mountain once—releasing our shame and settling into our worthiness, letting go of our facade and finding true belonging, becoming aware of the thing we're here to do and finally doing it—only to face a frustratingly similar view once again. For instance, as we practice our passion, our shame might get triggered unexpectedly. Or in a moment of vulnerability our belonging might suddenly be cast into doubt all over again. Or a newfound interest or a devastating disappointment may call our passion and our purpose into question once more.

That's okay.

It doesn't mean you've failed. It means you've *continued*. That's how the climb is supposed to go. You are simply seeing the same things from a little higher up. When this happens, it doesn't mean your story is over. It means it's time to write a sequel. And in each sequel, you'll release another piece of your shame, refine your community a little more, and become aware of a subtle nuance or new direction—perhaps even a new purpose—for your passion.

The good news is, gradually, as you write your sequels, the going will get a little easier, because you'll learn how to focus on the act you are in at any given time. You will learn—when it feels like you're living a little bit of each act all at once—to identify which act your soul is currently *most* engaged with, and you will get better and better at collecting your scattered energies and bringing them to bear upon the tasks of *that* act.

When, for example, out of nowhere, your shame picks up a megaphone and begins to drown out all of your other voices, including grace—*especially* grace—you'll recognize act one for what it is. You'll know right away you need to slow down, be still, breathe, and listen, waiting it out until the whisper of worthiness returns and you get to hear something new and good about your true self. Then, with a newfound assurance of the beautiful being you are, you'll go to your people and create even more beautiful belonging with them—even more vulnerability and tenderness, more grace and forgiveness, more sacrifice and compassion. And the cycle will go on.

Until, once again, you arrive where you started, and know yourself for the first time.

I remember reading the Harry Potter books for the first time.

The beloved characters. The relationships between them. The increasingly clear purpose of their arcing narrative. The inevitable march to the final showdown. The way love wins. The world of magic, with its own vocabulary, its schools, its culture and norms and mores, its shops and its commerce, its habits and its rhythms. It's a world I didn't want to leave, a story I didn't want to end.

I remember how slowly I turned the pages as the story neared its conclusion; the tenderness I felt as the pages at the front of the seventh book began to outnumber the pages at the back. I remember setting it down from time to time so I could savor it, because though

I felt an urge to rush through and find out how it all ended, I knew more than anything I just wanted to cherish it and to slow, slow, slow.

A life well told works the same way.

As your journey cycles upward toward the summit, you will retain some of the urgency of your youth—a part of you will desperately want to know how it all ends—but it is gradually replaced by *another* kind of urgency. It's an urgency that, paradoxically, leads to a slowing down. The urge to collect a bunch of experiences is replaced by an urge to dispense with distractions. The urge to be higher is replaced by an urge to be *here*—to take in the view that, with each step upward, is becoming increasingly vast and thus increasingly beautiful. More and more, you will be aware: the last page is coming, and your story will end.

More and more, you will want to pause the journey and *savor* it.

It's late afternoon, sometime in the spring of my fifth-grade year, not long after moving out of the trailer park and back to my hometown. My new best friend and I are playing in a field near his home in the country. The first part of the memory is shapeless and unformed. I can't remember exactly what we were doing, but I'm guessing we were playing like boys do—tossing a baseball, probably, and telling jokes we shouldn't have been telling. Like I said, the memory is hazy. Until it isn't.

The memory suddenly takes shape when we hear the yell.

From his house, somewhere over the hill, his mother is yelling his sister's name repeatedly. We look at each other and then we look in the direction of the house, and just as we're setting our sights on the hilltop, his little sister comes bursting over the horizon. She's only been walking for a few months, but she is moving *fast*. She has a smile plastered from one ear to the other, she's giggling with delight, and she's wearing nothing but a diaper. She runs toward us through the long prairie grass and it quickly becomes clear she just wants to join us. She is a soul wearing skin, and little else.

And she simply wants to play.

The years have come and gone, and with the years, many memories have slipped into my mental abyss. But *this* one. This one remains. The image of her cresting the hill is etched in my mind. I remember her mother hollering and I remember her bouncing toward us through the long grass and I remember thinking, "I want to be like her again."

By fifth grade, there was already a little one in me longing to be himself once again.

That was almost thirty years ago. My body has aged a lot in those years—it has an odd new shape, wrinkles where things used to be smooth, less hair than ever before, and the hair that's left is quickly fading to gray. The aging of my body isn't slowing down anytime soon.

Yet I've noticed, my soul seems to be aging in reverse.

I'm a little way up the mountain now, and I'm closer than ever to granting that little guy inside of me his wish from so long ago. My soul seems to be shedding weight. It's feeling more limber and agile than I can ever remember. It's gathering energy. And the spark within it is growing brighter, pushing back my darkness like a little kid running through a field pushing back grass, just wanting to play.

So here I am,

with this love letter,

knocking on your door,

as if it's late on a Friday afternoon,

sometime in the spring of our fifth-grade year,

knocking and asking,

Do you want to come out and play?

Acknowledgments

I've always been a bit of a rule follower, and conventional wisdom says in book acknowledgments you should only thank people who directly contributed to this particular book. However, seeing as this book arises out of an entire lifetime of experiences—and tells stories about quite a few of those—I figure by expressing some general gratitude I'm not breaking the rules, just *bending* them a little. So . . .

Mom and Dad—thank you for your quiet heroism in lifting our family up out of one story and into a better one. Kristi and Kyle—being younger siblings isn't always easy. Thank you for forgiving me all those years I tried to make you feel less than enough so I could feel like I was at least enough. My deepest gratitude to all the many friends and family who have been grace to me—thank you for seeing the good thing within me and reflecting it back to me, even when I couldn't see it in myself. And a special thanks in that regard to Vovô and Vuvu—you treated me like a grandson from the very first day your granddaughter introduced me to you, and you have loved me like that ever since. I've never had to wonder if I belong to you, and that is the greatest gift a young man can be given. I want to thank Judith and Merlin Willard—my high school English teachers—who cemented in me a deep love for literature and for writing. And finally, I want to thank every client I have seen over the years—you have taught me how to be courageous, and for that I am forever grateful.

Okay, enough rule bending.

I've learned a book comes to publication through a series of serendipities and generosities and the hard, hard work of many good and brilliant people. First, I want to thank Ken Phillips, who believed in me enough to show my work to his friend Philip Yancey. Thank you, Philip, for believing in me enough to connect me with your agent, Kathryn Helmers. Kathy, you took on a rookie and saved me thousands of dollars in writing conferences by single-handedly teaching me how to construct a book. Thank you for your patience, professionalism, and generosity. David Morris at Zondervan—thank you for taking a chance on a mostly unproven writer who doesn't fit easily into any particular box. Kim Tanner, my copyeditor, thank you for leaving no stone—or mixed metaphor—unturned; your keen eye brought clarity to every page. And my gratitude could not be deeper for my wise and wonderful editor, Sandra Vander Zicht. Sandy, I can't imagine what it was like to open up a first draft written by a guy who had previously only written disjointed, unrelated blog posts. You poured your wisdom and grace into this manuscript and made it whole. In that sense, you are the shalom in these pages.

Finally, I want to thank the people who supported, encouraged, and informed this book behind the scenes. Ben McCoy—thank you for loaning your professional expertise to a friend who had no idea what he was doing. You are always a source of calm and encouragement to me. A huge thank you to David Clinton—we opened up a therapy practice together in the middle of writing this book, and not once did you ask me to put the business before the manuscript. Thank you for always encouraging this passion of mine. To all of my lovely blog readers—and particularly those folks who have been a part of our Courtyard Conversations—thank you for being a safe space to think through these ideas in public. So many of the words in this book are as much yours as mine—I couldn't have done this without you.

And, of course, to my little ones and my wife—thank you for embracing the bizarre paradox that to write a book *to* you, *about* you, and *for* you, I needed to neglect you, sometimes for days at a time. Daddy's done now. Want to play?

Sources

CHAPTER 2: The Search for Healing in Our Relationships

Page 26 *"Love your neighbor"*: Matthew 22:39.

CHAPTER 3: The Search for Healing through Significance

Page 30 *"deemed very good"*: Genesis 1:31.

Page 30 *"knit together in your mother's womb"*: Psalm 139:13.

Page 30 *"the salt of the earth"*: Matthew 5:13–14.

CHAPTER 4: Healing in Three Acts

Page 42 *"At the heart of the universe . . ."*: Philip Yancey, *Disappointment with God: Three Questions No One Asks Aloud* (Grand Rapids: Zondervan, 1988), 55.

CHAPTER 8: The Difference Between Getting Rich and Living Richly

Page 79 *"The mass of men . . ."*: Henry David Thoreau, *Walden, Or, Life in the Woods* (Mineola, NY: Dover Publications, 1995), 4.

CHAPTER 10: The Good News That Sounds Too Good to Be True

Page 85 *"in a dream"*: Job 33:14–15.

Page 85 *"He will shelter you"*: Psalm 91:4 NLT.

Page 86 *"no program for this . . ."*: Thomas Merton, *Conjectures of a Guilty Bystander* (New York: Doubleday, 1968), 156.

Page 87 *"A wave of light . . ."*: Paul Tillich, *The Shaking of the Foundations* (New York: Scribner, 1948), 161–62.

CHAPTER 13: You Are a Somebody (and So Is Everybody Else)

Page 106 *"The human eye . . ."*: John O'Donohue, *Anam Cara: A Book of Celtic Wisdom* (New York: HarperCollins, 1998), 103.

CHAPTER 14: Why Loneliness Happens, How We Make It Worse, and What We Can Do to Make It Better

Page 117 *"a gentle whisper"*: 1 Kings 19:12.

CHAPTER 18: Maybe Heaven Really Is in Our Midst

Page 140 *"Let the little children come to me"*: Matthew 19:14.

Page 140 *"the kingdom of heaven is near"*: Matthew 10:7 NLT.

CHAPTER 20: The Most Painful Part of Finding Belonging

Page 150 *"It takes one person . . ."*: Lewis B. Smedes, *The Art of Forgiving: When You Need to Forgive and Don't Know How* (New York: Ballantine, 1997), 27.

CHAPTER 21: When Announcing Yourself Means Announcing Your Need

Page 156 *"No man is an island . . ."*: John Donne, *Devotions upon Emergent Occasions and Death's Duel* (New York: Vintage, 1999), 63.

CHAPTER 23: The Thing You Never Knew You Always Wanted to Do

Page 180 *"Lighthouses don't go running . . ."*: Anne Lamott, *Bird by Bird: Some Instructions on Writing and Life* (New York: Anchor, 1995), 225.

CHAPTER 28: The Redemptive Relationship Between Passion, Pain, and Purpose

Page 214 *"You have to learn to love . . ."*: "The Late, Great Stephen Colbert," *GQ*, August 17, 2015. http://www.gq.com/story/stephen-colbert-gq-cover-story.
Page 215 *"The place God calls . . ."*: Frederick Buechner, *Wishful Thinking: A Seeker's ABC* (San Francisco: HarperOne, 1993), 119.
Page 216 *"That is what mortals ..."*: C. S. Lewis, *The Great Divorce* (San Francisco: HarperOne, 2015), 69.

CHAPTER 29: A Peace That Surpasses All Understanding

Page 221 *"parts of a single body"*: 1 Corinthians 12:20.